J L Russell hails from South Wales, United Kingdom, leading to spending a part of his childhood days in Co Meath, Southern Ireland. From a young age, he admits to being creative and interested in just about everything; he was able to fill in life's repertoire. A few years later, after a heart-rending rollercoaster in his personal life, he turned his hand to writing.

This book is dedicated to the men and women who are or have been victims of domestic violence.

A moment of clarity, from J L Russell, "We, are not protecting our abuser anymore with stillness as they hide behind their smokescreen."

J L Russell

THE MULTIPLE LOVER

AUSTIN MACAULEY PUBLISHERS™

LONDON • CAMBRIDGE • NEW YORK • SHARJAH

A CIP catalogue record for this title is available from the British Library.

ISBN 9781528910101 (Paperback)
ISBN 9781528918060 (Hardback)
ISBN 9781528918565 (ePub e-book)

www.austinmacauley.com

First Published (2020)
Austin Macauley Publishers Ltd
25 Canada Square
Canary Wharf
London
E14 5LQ

Thanks to my pillars of strength from my supportive family and friends.

Chapter One

Work again! Being stuck in this dreary sales office day in and day out is just not how I had imagined my life. I feel like a hamster stuck on an endless wheel. *Great!* The screen freezes. Tapping like an ape at the keys for a few seconds might fix it. No, no it doesn't. Frustrated, I bang the keyboard of my computer. What the hell is wrong with this heap of shit now?

"Matt, I can hear you grinding your teeth from over here. Let me help."

My work colleague and best friend Lucy to the rescue! She hustles over to my desk with a swish of her floral skirt. "It will not work if you bang the keyboard like that. Let me have a look." She taps a few keys and just like that she has my computer purring like a kitten. "There you go. It just needed a little TLC." Lucy's smile matches her warm, comforting tone.

"Thanks, Lucy!" I say. "Speaking of TLC, I am waiting not so patiently for the intimate details of what went on this weekend!"

Lucy blushes. "Oh, well…"

"So? Come on, how did your weekend go? Did you meet the man of your dreams, or was he a troll?" I giggle. "Come on, show us a pic! He can't be that bad."

Lucy sighs and shows me a picture of a man on her phone.

I give my signature approval. "Mmm, he is definitely strawberries and cream! He would be at the top of my dessert menu." I love these conversations with Lucy; we are both hopeless romantics at heart, and sharing in each other's dating highs and lows are honestly the highlights of my dreary days stuck in this hellhole of an office. "So, did you get his number? When are you seeing him again? Come on, Lucy, don't leave me in suspense. You know I need this to get through the day." I give my friend full puppy-dog eyes, which I know she can't resist.

Finally, she starts to spill. "No, I didn't get his number. He said he would call me," she sighs.

Unfortunately, I am a person not blessed with a brain to mouth filter, so I blurt without thinking, "Yeah, the call that never comes!" *Shit! Why did I say that? Come on Matt think, think.* "I mean…aw, hun, you know you should never say goodbye until you have their number." That's all I can muster before the office door flies open.

"Here she comes, the witch with more awful shoes than her attitude," I whisper before our office manager, Jessica Ramscock, gets within earshot. She is the reason my heart sinks every time I enter this ruin of a workplace.

"Mr Storm, how is it remotely possible that you have time for gossip when the deadlines for the accounts are this afternoon? Get it done! I expect the report on my desk by 3 p.m., not one minute later!" She clips away on her high heels to go nag somebody else.

I'm pretty sure Jessica was the inspiration for Cruella de Vil. "She needs a bloody good shag, not the accounts report," I say to Lucy, who still looks shaken from Hurricane Jessica's brief, but no less destructive, visit to our desks. Once my humour wears off, I quickly realise my workload just got a lot heavier. Thanks a lot, Jessica.

"Come on, Matt, let's go get some lunch. My treat." Lucy, my angel, always knows just what to say.

When we arrive at the coffee shop, Lucy asks, "What do you fancy? I can't decide."

I start to peruse the menu, but my eyes are drawn a very handsome assistant, who is arranging a fresh batch of cakes in the counter display. My reply is out of my mouth before I really have a chance to think. "Well, I'm thinking five feet eight inches, blue eyes…"

"Matt! Not the eye candy assistant. I meant food. Come on, I'm starving."

The gorgeous sales assistant finishes his task and asks Lucy and me what we would like to order. I can't decide—my eyes are drawn to his fit body and I imagine him naked standing there in front of me. I am pulled back to reality when Lucy nudges my arm. The sales assistant says, "If you can't decide, I highly recommend the BLT sandwich. I'm Tom, by the way."

Lucy takes his advice and orders a BLT. I try to speak, but my tongue has stopped working. Tom is so mesmerising. I imagine us on a beach, with me rubbing sun lotion on his back.

Tom says, "And what can I get for you sir?"

My mouth finally decides to function. "I will have the same thing she is having!" I blurt out.

Tom walks off to the other side of the shop and prepares our sandwiches. Lucy looks at her watch. "Shit, is that the time? We are going to be late back to the office!"

"Oh, forget it," I say. "We give half our life to that place. Besides, being late once in a while is not the crime of the century. Ever thought of having a career change, hun?" I think I'm saying that last sentence to myself as much as to Lucy. When I was younger, I wanted to run a toyshop. I should've done that instead of accepting a dreary office job.

Tom returns and my ability to form words disappears once again. I take the sandwiches out of his hands, looking deep into his eyes. He gives me a wink; my body tingles all over. Lucy thanks Tom, but her voice sounds distant; everything except Tom fades into the background.

Lucy has to practically steer me away from the counter. As we are about to leave the shop, I have one more glance backwards, hoping Tom does not see me staring. Our eyes meet like two strangers in the dark. It's electric—I never want to stop looking at him.

In my distraction, I bump into Lucy, then fall over the sandwich board, knocking it to the ground. Lucy tries to help me set it back up and Tom leaps from behind his counter to assist. "Hey, don't worry. People are always knocking this thing over." He chuckles. I feel as if I could just die of embarrassment on the spot.

A loud clap of thunder splits the air and a bolt of lightning lights up the darkening sky. "Come on, Matt, we are going to be so late!" Lucy snaps me to my senses.

"Just one second, Lucy." I stare at Tom as he bends over to repair the sandwich board I knocked over. His bum is so tight in his trousers that it indents his underwear lining. As Lucy drags me back to the office, I have to hide the sudden movement in my trousers.

We finally arrive back at the office, soaking wet from the thunderstorm. Lucy stares down at my damp trousers. "Someone got all excited!"

"Piss off. You're just jealous that he is most likely on my bus, not yours!" We both laugh as we scoff our sandwiches down in the entryway.

As I bite into the BLT sandwich Tom's hands made, a glob of ketchup flies out of the bread and into Lucy's face. She screams and glares at me, her face and parts of her blouse covered in red sauce. "Matt!"

I can't help it; I burst into laughter.

"Not funny," she says, but she smiles too. "Not the worst thing I've had all over my face."

I snigger and dig a pack of tissues out of my pocket. "Here."

She wipes the ketchup off her face and begins to dab at her blouse, but it just smears it around. She sighs. "Can you grab me some water?"

I fetch her a cupful from the water fountain, but as I hand it to her, she fumbles and it spills all over her blouse. Lucy's bra appears like a magic trick through her blouse. She gasps so theatrically that I can't control my laughter. "I'm so sorry, Lucy! I'll get you some paper towels."

"You had better, Matt! Now my breasts are on show for all to see."

I manage to find her a roll of toilet paper—not as good as paper towels, but it'll do—and we finish our lunch without further incident. Luckily, Lucy's blouse has mostly dried by the time we finish eating.

We'll need lots of energy to face the Wicked Witch of the East, Jessica, during the sales meeting later this afternoon.

As we head back to our desks, I still can't stop thinking of Tom from the coffee shop. I look at the clock on the wall and it's showing 3:05 p.m. "Oh shit!" I say to Lucy. "I am late for the meeting, and Jessica will have my balls on a spear." Why did I waste so much time being distracted by a hot man? I grab the files I need and run like a dog chasing a hare through the office corridors, my heart beating faster as I run. At last, I approach the meeting room, with my heart ready to jump out of my chest. I hesitate before opening the door—I hear voices behind it. *Fuck. The meeting has started.* I straighten my tie, take a deep breath as if it's my last and open the meeting room door. The voices hush.

Jessica stares at me as if I'm something disgusting she trod in with her bargain box shoes from the local market. I look around the table at all of the company directors and feel their eyes piercing me. I want the ground to open and swallow me up on the spot.

Jessica coughs. "So glad you could join us, Mr Storm. I presume you have the file I asked you for?" She glances pointedly at her watch.

"Yes, I do have the file. I'm so sorry, everybody, I—"

"Just sit down, Mr Storm."

I hurry over to the nearest empty chair, apologising in a soft voice to the rest of the board. I sit down to open the file Jessica asked me to prepare before lunchtime.

Jessica says, "Now, shall we continue with the rest of the business at hand? First up on the agenda…"

I sit there and listen to God Almighty Jessica Ramscock preach about how we need to boost the company's revenue. I try to concentrate, but Tom sneaks his way back into my mind. My eyes wander around the room, imagining one of the directors as Tom. The things I would love to get up to with him! I close my eyes to further explore my fantasy, but I am brought back to reality when Jessica slams her hands on the table and says, "What ideas do you have, Mr Storm, to boost extra revenue?"

I gasp and say, "Sexy pants."

The stares from the directors pierce my soul and Jessica looks ready to blow her top. I sink down in the chair. "Um…uh…Jessica, may I be excused? Something has come over me and I feel unwell."

"Very well, Mr Storm."

I give my apologies to the room and take a slow walk back to my desk; my mind is unable to focus on anything. When I arrive, Lucy is there waiting. "So, how did the sales meeting go?" she asks.

I roll my eyes. "Jessica is trying to impress the board and become the queen of Gallagher & Masons."

Lucy laughs. "I doubt that. She thinks she's already the queen."

"Very true. Come on, let's get the hell out of this prison. I think you will agree we have done our time for one day."

On the way home, I ask, "Do you fancy a little window shopping?"

Lucy smiles. "Window shop…this wouldn't happen to be an excuse to visit the coffee shop, would it?"

"Wow! Lucy, you have read my mind. If you ever left Gallagher & Masons, you could easily get a job as a psychic."

As we get closer, I realise that all the lights are out in the coffee shop and I have missed my hunk. Lucy says, "Never mind, Matt. There's always next time. But you have put me in the mood now to do clothes shopping."

"Okay," I say to Lucy. "Let's see what's hot and what's not!" I could sure use some retail therapy to get over my disappointment at not seeing Tom again.

We arrive at the shops and Lucy immediately spots a dress she likes in a window. "Come on, let's go in! I want to try this on!"

"Hang on," I say as she physically drags me into the store in a fit of excitement. "You're as mad as a box of frogs!"

Lucy heads off to try the dress on and I find a chair close to the dressing room entrance to sit in while I read through my messages on my phone.

Lucy pops her head out of the dressing room curtain. "What do you think?"

I nearly fall off of my chair in laughter—she has tucked her knickers into the dress's blue material. Lucy starts to laugh along with me and then looks down at the dress. "I don't think it's me. What do you think, Matt?"

"Well, it's you who has to wear it, not me."

Lucy decides the dress is not for her and hands it back to the shop assistant. As we leave, I hear a clinking sound and I turn around to see my car keys lying on the ground. They must have fallen out of my pocket. I bend down to pick them up and a pair of shoes appears near my face. A voice says, "Let me help you with those."

My hand brushes the stranger's hand as I glance up. I cannot believe my eyes; it's Tom from the coffee shop!

My knees go weak as Tom picks up my car keys. I slowly stand up and find myself staring into his beautiful blue eyes. *This is it, Matt. Go in for the kill! Ask him out—you know you want to!* But I can't—my mouth refuses to work.

Tom hands me my keys. "Hey, you were in Cappuccino's at lunch time, right?"

"Um…uh…" It's no good. My brain is a useless lump around him.

"Oh yeah, that was us," Lucy butts in, pushing me backward before I can embarrass myself further.

Tom says, "Yeah, I remember you. Two BLTs."

I hold on to the shop awning's post to stop myself from falling.

"Well, it's nice to meet you outside of work. I'm Tom—dunno if I said that already." When he shakes my hand, I feel like a bolt of electricity has gone through me. He continues speaking. "I'm afraid I have to rush; I have an appointment I have to attend. But before I go, I'd like to ask—how would you like to go for a drink sometime?"

I can't believe it! He actually just asked me out! But Lucy steps in front of me and says, "We would love to!"

Tom smiles and looks down at me. "I mean...I don't mean to be rude, but..."

I finally regain my powers of speech and say to Lucy, "I think he means just me and him!"

"Oh, sorry," Lucy says. "Three's a crowd, I suppose." She walks off in a huff like a puff of smoke.

"Lucy..." I begin to call after her, but Tom touches my arm.

"So, about that drink," he says.

"Sure, yeah, I'd love to," I say, staring after Lucy. As hot as Tom is, I can't lose my best friend over him. "Looks like I've got to run." I start speed-walking to try and catch up with her.

Tom shouts, "How about I meet you at O'Sheas tomorrow night at 8:00 p.m.?"

I glance back at him, happiness bubbling up in my chest. "See you then!"

I break into a run to catch up with Lucy, excited as a kid with a new toy at the thought of my date with Tom tomorrow night.

I finally reach her on the steps of the car park entrance. She stares into space, her hair moving gently in the breeze.

"You know, if the wind changes, you will stay like that," I say, wrapping my arms around her. She looks like she could use a hug.

She pouts. "I will never find a man."

I give her a kiss on the cheek. "Mr Right is out there somewhere. You will find him someday, hun. Come on, let's go home."

Lucy kisses me back on the cheek and composes herself, and we both head off to our cars.

Driving home, I am buzzing like a bumblebee. My date with sexy Tom is only twenty-four hours away. It's exciting, but also nerve-wracking. What if he doesn't like me once he gets to know me? Maybe best not to think about the negatives—it'll only make me more nervous.

My mum is reading a book on the sofa when I arrive home. "Evening, Mum!" I say, heading towards the stairs.

"Evening, Matt, love! What do you fancy for tea?"

"It's okay, Mum. I will have something later." I dash upstairs to my bedroom, where I open my wardrobe in search of something to wear for my date tomorrow night. I look through every single article of clothing I own, pulling hanger after hanger off the rack, hoping something will jump out at me to wear. At last, I find a T-shirt I haven't worn in ages. I walk over to my mirror on the back of my door as I try the T-shirt on. I am so determined to make this T-shirt fit me, even if I'll look like the Incredible Hulk in it! All the better for Tom to see my muscle definition.

In the end, the shirt proves to be perfectly flattering. As I am taking it off, I hear a loud scream and a stomping like a herd of elephants coming towards my bedroom door. It bursts open and I am knocked against the wall of my bedroom with one arm out of the T-shirt and the other still in it. My sister Loraine runs around my bedroom, screaming, "Mum, Matt, help! There's a large spider in the bathroom!"

My heart thumps from the shock of her intrusion and I can feel a bruise rising on my shoulder from where I hit the wall. "You stupid cow!" I yelp. "You could have broken my arm!"

My mother shouts from the hall, "What in the bloody hell are the pair of you doing up there?"

I pull my T-shirt fully off and realise it's torn from the force of my sister crashing into my bedroom. *Oh, bollocks, bollocks, it's ruined! Thank you very much, Sis.* I throw the T-shirt down on my bed. "I wanted to wear this for my date tomorrow night." I sit down angrily on the mattress and clench the shirt in my hand.

My mother steps into the room. "Don't worry, Matt, I can fix this for you." She takes the crumpled-up T-shirt out of my hand. "I will have it looking brand new in no time. Now, Loraine, where is this spider you saw love?"

My mother and sister leave me in peace and my frustration ebbs away. Mum really is amazing—I know she'll make my shirt look good as new. Now, it's time for me to hit the hay. I have a big day ahead of me tomorrow.

As the sun wakes me up, I jump out of bed and open my curtains, feeling so excited about the thought of my date with Tom tonight. I quickly get dressed and whistle as I make my way to the bathroom. I have a quick wash and shave and clean my teeth, and then I dance myself down the stairs to the sound of an empty house. Everyone else must have gone to work already. I see there's a note on the kitchen table from my mother, telling me she has repaired my T-shirt and placed it on the back of a dining room chair for me. I head for the dining room and pluck the shirt from the back of the chair. As well as repairing it, Mum has washed and ironed it. The fabric smells like a bunch of roses in an orchard and it looks like I never tore it.

I am one happy guy as I make my way out the front door. The birds are singing and the sun is shining; nothing will spoil my day.

As I close my front door, I glance over at our neighbour, Shirley, who is cleaning her windows with a bucket of soapy water and a sponge. She looks over and spots me. "Morning, Matt! What a lovely morning it is."

Any morning is a good one when you have a date with a hot man later. I reply in an elated tone, "It sure is, Shirley!"

I must have sounded too enthusiastic, because Shirley puts her bucket down, heads over to me and starts talking about her grandchildren, gesticulating so wildly that drops of water fly off her rubber gloves. "So my lovely Hannah, she's turning twelve and she's always showing me these filter things on her phone that do the most ridiculous things to your face! There was one that turned me into a cat. I'm telling you, technology these days is just…"

I let her ramble on and my thoughts wander to imagining what my sexy Tom will be wearing for our date. When Shirley appears to have exhausted her supply of grandchildren stories, I say goodbye to her and she returns to cleaning her windows.

I'm desperate to see Tom again; I don't know if I can wait for tonight. But maybe I don't have to wait.

I get into my car and start the engine. The radio blasts out the song *Tonight Is Going to Be a Good Night*. Just as I reverse off my drive, my phone beeps. It's a text from Lucy, asking if I want to meet her for some breakfast at Rosie's Cafe before we go to work. I text back and tell her I am stuck in traffic and can't meet her or else I'll be late for work.

I arrive at the town centre car park and take my ticket from the pay machine. I look down and there is a young homeless guy wearing shabby clothes and holding a pot with a few coins inside. I reach into my pocket, find a £5 note and place it in his tin. "Here you go. Buy yourself some breakfast."

He smiles and grabs his pot to see how much money he has already collected.

I smile and carry on, walking down the car park steps towards the office. But I have a quick stop to make on the way.

As the coffee shop comes into view, Tom is just setting up the sandwich board out front. I walk faster so I don't miss him. My heart thuds as I get closer.

He looks up and a radiant smile spreads across his face. I can't help but beam back at him. "Morning," we say at the exact same time and then chuckle.

"You go first," he says.

"No, you go first," I mimic. Then, more seriously, I continue, "Morning, Tom. How are you today?"

Tom replies, "I am good, thanks for asking. Matt, isn't it?"

My name coming from his lips makes my brain go all mushy again. I stutter out, "Yeah, and you're Tom." Ugh, that has to have been the least intelligent thing I could have said. I try to cover it up by adding, "Are we still on for that drink at O'Sheas tonight?"

"Yeah, of course. Looking forward to it."

"Me too," I reply. "Why don't we exchange numbers?"

Tom reaches inside his apron, which serves to draw my eyes to his crotch. All I can think about is what's lying hidden beneath his underwear. I force my gaze away from his groin as he brings out his phone. He begins, "My number is—"

"Hold on a minute, I need to get mine. It's in my coat pocket." I grab my phone and see there is a text from Lucy asking where I am. I'll deal with that later—first things first. "Okay, ready."

Tom recites his number, and as he does, I carefully enter it into my phone. "Let me call you now," I say, pressing the button with the telephone icon. I hear Tom's phone vibrate in his hand.

"Cool," he says. "I have your number. A priceless treasure."

My cheeks flush as my own phone begins to vibrate. I look at the screen; it's Lucy calling. I press the 'deny call' button and shoot her a quick text. *I'm on my way to the office, I promise.* Who cares if I'm late for work? I hate that job anyway.

"You're in high demand this morning," Tom says with a laugh.

A couple of old ladies pass by. "Excuse me, young man," one of them says to Tom, "but are you open?"

Tom replies, "We sure are."

The ladies head into the shop. "I think that's our cue to go to work," I say.

Tom smiles at me. "Yeah, I'd better give these pensioners their daily caffeine."

"Yeah." And I'd better make a move too, since I will be in hot water for being late. Totally worth it, though. "I will see you tonight at 8 p.m. at O'Sheas."

"See you then!" Tom waves as he goes into the shop to serve the old ladies.

I am so happy as I make my way to work. I feel like I am on cloud nine. Nothing will spoil my day! I glance at my watch; it's almost 9:30 a.m.

"Fuck," I mutter, breaking into a run. I didn't realise just how late I am. My phone starts to ring again. It's Lucy.

I answer, out of breath. "Hello?" The office building looms ahead. Almost there.

"Matt! You're so major late. Jessica wants you to report to her office the minute you arrive. Where've you been? The traffic can't possibly have been that bad."

I don't want her to know—she got so upset when Tom asked me out yesterday that I think telling her the truth will only make her huffy again. "I have just arrived. See you soon." I hang up before she can say anything else.

I make my way into the office reception, saying a breathless good morning to Vera and Steve—the receptionist and security guard. The lift opens, I run into it and press the button for the tenth floor. It seems to take forever to reach my destination.

At last, the doors slide open and I bolt out into the hallway. As I do, I bump into Molly, the drinks lady who is doing her morning rounds.

"Sorry, Molly!" I say. "I am late."

She pulls a sour face. "You got a train to catch this bloody morning? Hell, what's wrong with you?"

I throw another apology over my shoulder as I run down the corridor. Finally, I arrive at my desk. My angel and best friend, Lucy, waits for me with a cuppa; my computer is all started up and ready for me to hit the keys.

Lucy hands me the tea. "Why are you so late, Matt?"

I suppose I was planning on keeping my visit to Tom a secret, but I shouldn't keep secrets from my best friend. She deserves to know. "I had to take a sudden detour on the way to work," I say, smiling at her.

"This sudden detour wouldn't happen to work in a coffee shop, would he?"

I giggle a little. "Maybe." I draw my eyebrows together. "You're not upset at me, are you?"

"Of course not. I'm happy for you." She grins and I know we're okay again. "Now go on—you better face Cruella de Vil! She is in a foul mood, so tread carefully."

"Carefully is my middle name." I hold up my cup of tea in a toast and drink it down before making my way to Jessica's office.

Jessica's fingers tap impatiently against the arm of her chair as I enter. "Mr Storm, would you explain to me why you are so late for work?"

I have to think of something good. I can't say I went to see Tom. As I rack my brains, the image of the shabby young man in the car park flashes into my head. "I had to help a homeless person," I say.

Jessica stares at me for a few more seconds, then leaps out of her chair, making me jump. "You have just given me a wonderful idea. Yes, a splendid idea." Her face softens—as much as a wicked witch's face can soften, anyway. "I'll let you off this time, Mr Storm. But don't be late again, or I'll have to dock your wages."

I would like to see her try to reduce my pay. I do enough extra hours in this workhouse as it is. After reading me the company policy on lateness—which I privately refer to as Chapter Sixty-Nine of the Ramscock Bible—Jessica tells me to return to my desk and carry on with my work.

I make my way back to my desk and Lucy raises her eyebrows at me. "Well? How did it go?"

"I am still in shock. When I went into her office, it was almost as if she was ready to explode. I had to make up a reason why I was late. When she heard it, she totally changed her tune. She said I'd given her a brilliant idea and let me off with a slap on the wrist."

Lucy laughs. "Matt, if you fell in shit, you would come out smelling like roses."

I chuckle along with her, but then my phone beeps and a wave of apprehension cuts off my mirth. "Who could be texting me at this time of morning?" *What if it's Tom texting to cancel our date? I knew he was way too hot to be interested in someone like me.*

"You won't know until you look," Lucy says.

My fingers are like jelly as I fish my phone out of my pocket.

"Well?" Lucy moves to look over my shoulder. "Is it from Mr Wonderful Tom?"

"Hang on." I angle the phone away from her and unlock my screen to find it's not a text at all—it's an email from Jessica, reminding me of what she had discussed with me in my lateness meeting. As the mingled disappointment and relief at not receiving a message from Tom hits me, another email from Jessica pops up in my inbox. This one is addressed to all employees, informing us that she wants us all to bring a tin of food for homeless people in to work within the next few weeks.

"Now, that's unexpected," I say to Lucy. "Jessica, doing something nice for the community? Next thing we know, she'll be giving us all a pay raise!"

Lucy smiles. "Don't get your hopes up. Feeding the poor of Kelford may be out of character for her, but pay raises are flat-out ridiculous."

My phone beeps again with a message from Tom. My gut twists—this must be the cancellation text I feared.

I open the text. It's practically an essay, beginning with, *Hi, Matt! Sorry for bothering you, but I just can't stop thinking about you. How is your day going so far?* My nervousness flips around into joy. He's not breaking it off at all!

"What is it?" Lucy manoeuvres herself to try and snoop at my screen.

"I am still reading it! Hang on." My smile gets wider and wider with every word I devour. Tom finishes his text by saying, *Looking forward to tonight*, with a smile emoji and a kiss to top it all off.

I read the text to Lucy, who starts singing 'Love Is in the Air'.

I laugh at her. "Don't get too excited. It's just a drink." I'm not sure whether I'm saying it more to her, or to myself.

At that moment, both our office phones ring. Looks like it's back to the grind.

As I type away, I am counting down the time on the office clock, willing it to hurry up and get to 5 p.m. When there's just one hour to go, Lucy leaves her desk and asks if I want a coffee.

"Yes, please. With two sugars and lots of milk!" It's happy hour now. Just sixty more minutes and it's action stations to get myself all dolled up for Tom. What better way to celebrate than with a hot drink?

Lucy heads to the staff room to make our final cuppa of the day. As I work on my last account, a hand touches my left shoulder and I almost jump out of my skin. I twist around and it's Lewis, our very own Postman Pat and office clown of Gallagher & Masons. "Bloody hell, Lewis, you want to be careful of that!"

He looks confused. "What do you mean?"

"Creeping up on people from behind!"

He laughs. "Who else did you think it could be?"

"Well, with all the zombies who work in this place, it could have been anyone, I suppose."

"I'm no zombie. I'm a bona fide vampire." Lewis holds his index fingers next to his mouth in an impression of fangs. "Anyway, I just wanted to ask if I could borrow a pen."

I pass him a blue biro from the pot next to my computer. Lucy returns with two cups of coffee and sets mine down on the desk.

Lewis says, "Hey, where's mine?"

Lucy pulls a face. "It's in the staff room in the kettle and the mug is on the sink."

Lewis humphs. "You two will think twice about denying me coffee when I come drink your blood later." He grins, wiggles his 'fangs' next to his mouth again and sashays off with my pen.

The clock strikes 5 p.m. and I resist the urge to pump my fist in the air. "Come on, Lucy. Let's get out of here."

She replies, "Sorry, I have catching up to do. But I will meet you in the morning at the car park so you can tell me all about your wonderful night with sexy Tom."

"Deal. See you tomorrow!" I jump from my chair like a frog leaping from lily pad to lily pad. My nerves buzz as I enter the lift full of work colleagues, some of whom apparently don't know what a can of deodorant is. The smell is unbearable. Lewis grins at me from across the cramped space. I will the lift to hurry up and let us off already.

Suddenly, the lift judders, the lights flicker and we stop moving. Everyone groans. "Oh, for fuck's sake," I mutter.

Everybody reaches inside their coats and bags for their mobiles. I do the same, hoping to alert Lucy, who is still at her desk. But I don't have any reception and the Wi-Fi doesn't reach through the metal walls.

"It's no good, I have no signal," I say to the lady next to me.

"Press the bloody alarm!" someone yells.

If I can't get out of this lift soon, I'll have to kiss my date with Tom goodbye. My palms begin to sweat. Who knows when I'll get another opportunity to go out with such a hot guy? Maybe I'm doomed to be single forever.

Lewis says, "Shall I tell a joke?"

"No!" we all shout.

The temperature rises as all the bodies turn it into a human sauna. I try not to think about how much sweat everyone's producing right now. God, this is disgusting.

The time stretches on and on. The air becomes stifling. I cover my nose and mouth to try and block the smell, but it doesn't work. Someone says that the maintenance crew is working on getting us unstuck, but I wish they'd bloody hurry up. The minutes turn into an hour, then two hours. Shit, shit, shit.

At last, the lift judders and moves down again. Everybody cheers and I let out a whoop. I'll have my date after all! But only just—the time on my phone says 7:00 p.m. I only have an hour to get ready!

The lift reaches the ground floor and everyone races to get through the twin metal doors as if they were entering a January sale. I push my way through my sweaty work colleagues. "Excuse me, please. Excuse me."

Bursting out of the lift and into the cool air of the foyer is the best feeling in the world, but I don't have time to enjoy it. I run like the clappers down the office steps and along the high street, all way to the car park.

When I reach the car park, I am in two minds—take the lift and catch my breath, or stick with the stairs? The thought of being in another lift makes my chest constrict, so I take a deep breath and begin my task of reaching the fifth floor where my car is parked. I stop several times to rest; I have a stitch in my stomach from all this exertion.

At last, I pay my parking charge at the pay station and proceed to my car. The time on my dashboard is showing 7:20 p.m. I need to move. I quickly reverse the car out of the parking space and make my way home.

I arrive home, not bothering to park the car on the drive. I open the car door and begin to undress as I run up the garden path, removing my tie and unbuttoning my shirt, hoping none of the neighbours see me. As I enter the house, a voice from the kitchen shouts, "Matt, is that you?"

"No, it's the milkman," I reply.

My mother comes from the kitchen with a cup of coffee and my T-shirt over her arm. "Here you go, Matt. I was just making a cuppa and thought you might like one. Help you put your feet up after work. And here's your T-shirt… I don't want it cluttering up the dining room any longer."

"Thanks, Mum." I take the T-shirt off her and accept the steaming mug. I won't have time to finish the entire thing, but it seems rude to refuse outright when she's already made it for me. I take a few sips…the caffeine will do me good.

My mum clasps her hands together. "Now, tell me all about your day at work. You hardly ever talk about it. I want to know everything!"

"Sorry, but I haven't got time to talk. I am so late." I doubt she wants to hear about how much I hate my job anyway. I am so late. Like a bat out of hell, I run up the stairs to my bedroom. My phone pings in my trouser pocket. It's a text from Tom, saying he has arrived at the pub and he will be seated near the bar.

I text back, *I will leave mine in ten.*

He replies almost immediately with *Okay*, plus a kiss emoji. A rush of happiness goes through me.

After dumping my sweaty clothing in the laundry basket, I throw on a bathrobe and dash to the bathroom. The door refuses to budge. I hear singing from inside. It's my sister, Loraine.

I knock on the door. "Loraine? I need to have a wash!"

The singing continues.

I knock louder; she shouts from the other side of the door, "What?"

"How long are you going to be in there, Loraine? I need to use the shower."

"I've only just gotten in the bath."

"Can I come in for a quick wash and shave? I'll only be five minutes. Just put a towel around yourself. Please, Loraine!"

I hear nothing more from her. My request must have fallen on deaf ears, submerged in a bubble bath!

My first date with Tom and I will stink like a skunk! I run into my bedroom, strip naked and pour half a bottle of aftershave over myself from top to toe. I sing the words to the song *Tonight Will Be a Good Night*, more for luck than anything else. I don a pair of black boxers, the T-shirt my mother repaired and a pair of jeans. I splash more aftershave on myself and look in the mirror. Hopefully Tom likes the mussed-up look. "Let's hit the town!" I say to my reflection.

As I leave the bedroom, I am met on the landing by Loraine, who is clad in a fluffy bathrobe with her hair wrapped in a towel. "The bathroom is free now," she says.

"Too late now; I have to go." I run downstairs and grab my jacket off the coat hook. "I am off now, Mum!" I shout towards the living room. "See you later!"

"Wait, Matt, let me have a look at you!" My mother bustles out of the living room, looks me up and down and fixes the back of my jacket, as the collar is not straight. She kisses me on the cheek. "Have a lovely night, Matt." Either she doesn't notice the overwhelming smell of aftershave, or she's polite enough not to mention it.

"Thanks, Mum." I open the front door and walk down the drive.

My mother calls, "Matt, you have left your car keys!"

"Whoops!" I quickly run back and take the key from her as she stands in the doorway to see me off. I look back and wave to her, then I get in the car and drive off to the O'Sheas bar to meet Tom.

Chapter Two

I arrive at the car park just over the road from O'Sheas and as I check my appearance in the mirror of the car, nervousness and excitement start to bubble up inside me.

I look over at the battered old bus shelter; in the light of the street lamp, I see a guy and girl making out before their bus arrives. Maybe that's going to be me and Tom in few hours.

I have waited a whole twenty-four hours for this date with Tom and I don't want to mess it up. I get out of my car, lock the doors and take a slow walk across the road to the bar. It seems really busy in there. I walk around the side of the building and have a look through the window, trying to get a peek at the area where Tom said he would be sitting. I can't see much—a lot of people are blocking my view. Then, someone shifts and I am able to see the seats near the bar. There is no sign of Tom! My heart pounds. Where is he? I take my phone out of my pocket to see if he's texted me, but there's nothing. Maybe he had second thoughts and decided to scarper before I arrived.

I really don't know what to do. Do I go into the bar, or do I go back to my car and sit, hoping he will send me a text?

My phone rings and I jab my finger onto the accept call button without checking who it is. "Tom!"

"Guess again," Lucy's voice says.

"Oh. Hi, Lucy." I sag.

"How's your night going? You sound upset."

"I think Tom has gone. I've got no mates. I'm just alone waiting outside the bar, peering in through the window."

"You should go in. Tom might have gone to the toilet or to the smoking area."

Of course—she's right. That could very well be the explanation. "Thanks, hun. I did not think of that. I just assumed he'd left."

Lucy laughs. "Whatever would you do without me honey bee?"

"Not much." I smile. "Thanks. I'll see you at work on Monday."

I hang up, put my phone back into my coat pocket and enter the bar. A crowd of ladies on a hen night surge past. One of them apologises for nearly bumping into me as she holds up the bride, who seems to have had one too many.

When I reach the bar, I stand and have a look around, scanning the crowd for Tom. After a few minutes of fruitless searching, I sink down on a barstool. The barman asks me what I would like to drink.

"Pint of lager, please." Might as well drown my disappointment with a drink.

Someone taps me on the shoulder, and I turn to see Tom's smiling blue eyes. Blood rushes to my face. "I was starting to think you'd left!"

Tom laughs. "I would never leave you. How long have you been here?"

"Few minutes."

"Gosh, I'm sorry about that. I was out in the smoking area, having a cigarette."

I smile. "Well, that's a relief!"

"Do you often get stood up?" His eyes twinkle.

"Usually not." I really want to find out more about this sexy hunk of a man that's standing beside me in the flesh. I glance around the bar for an empty table where we can talk and get to know each other.

"Would you like a drink?" Tom asks.

"I have just ordered one. Can I get you a drink?"

"Yeah, sure. I will have a pint of lager."

"Snap! That's what I ordered!"

"Aha! Looks like we'll get along well." Tom turns his face away and wipes his nose. His eyes appear to be watering a bit. The smell of my aftershave must be quite overpowering to him. My face flushes even hotter, out of embarrassment this time. Why couldn't Loraine have gotten out of the bathroom quicker? I'll be a virgin forever at this rate.

The barman sets down my lager and I ask for a second one for Tom.

"So, do you come to O'Sheas often?" Tom asks.

"Sometimes." In truth, this is my first time in the place and I can't believe how busy it is.

Tom apologises again for running late, and I say, "Hey, no problem. I was running late too. You would not believe how my day at work ended."

The barman brings Tom's pint of lager. Tom tilts his head to one side as he looks at me. "Tell me more?"

Just then, I notice a couple getting up from their small table. The two now-empty chairs seem to beckon me. "Want to sit down?" I say to Tom.

Tom follows my gaze to the table and he slides off his barstool. "Sure."

He leads the way in his bum-tight jeans. His form-fitting T-shirt displays his muscles. Have I died and gone to heaven? He's so fit! I can't believe I am on a date with him.

Once we sit down, Tom asks me to carry on about how my day ended. I open my mouth to tell him about getting stuck in the lift, but the doors burst open and a huge wave of people a stag party?—enter the bar. The volume in the room increases and it is impossible to hear either of us talk.

I shout to Tom, "Shall we drink this and head somewhere else?"

Tom nods and we both down our pints. He yells to me, "I am just going for a ciggy."

"I will wait for you outside."

Tom heads off to the smoking area, while I make my way out of the bar door.

As I am waiting outside for Tom, the group of ladies of the hen party crash through the door. One throws a pink feather boa around me and dances in front me. "You're coming home with me!" she purrs, caressing my face with a long pink nail.

31

I stand still while another shoves an inflatable penis in my face. "Go on suck on this!" she slurs, tottering on her high heels. I shrug and they apparently decide my reactions aren't fun enough, so they decide to move on to somewhere else.

Fifteen minutes pass and Tom doesn't make a reappearance. What the hell is taking him so long? What if he didn't like me and decided to leave?

Finally, the door opens and Tom appears. "Sorry I took so long! I bumped into someone I hadn't seen in a long time and got chatting."

"No worries at all," I say.

"So Matt, what do you fancy doing now that we're out of that noise factory?"

I shrug. "I am easy."

He laughs. "What about a club? Or something to eat? Your choice."

Truth be told, I don't want either of those choices, I want to see the body behind the clothes. I want to skip first base and get to second. I want to explore his hot body and kiss those cherry lips of his. But I suspect he wants to go clubbing. What do I say? I don't want to make the wrong decision. He might end our date early if I do that. I have to think.

Maybe I don't have to make the choice myself. I say to Tom, "Let's toss a coin. Heads means we go clubbing; tails means we find another pub."

"Okay then," Tom says.

I take a coin out of my pocket and throw it up in the air. It lands on tails.

"Pub it is," Tom says. Is he disappointed? I can't tell.

I smile. "Shall we go to the Melford Arms pub?"

"Lead the way." He sounds happy enough, so hopefully he doesn't mind not going to a club.

"I need to bring the car over."

"Leave it there. The Melford Arms is just up the road."

We walk off to the pub, discussing our jobs as we go. But when we arrive, we find it closed.

"Oh, bollocks," I say.

"Never mind," Tom says. "It's getting late. Maybe it's best if we call it a night."

I feel like a boat on the ocean which has had the wind blown out of its sails. I want to spend as much time with Tom as possible, but I suppose that isn't happening today. I say, "Yeah, maybe that's for the best. I have a few plans tomorrow and I have to be up early."

Tom replies, "That's a shame. I was going to ask you if you wanted to go for dinner tomorrow night."

My stomach does a somersault. On the outside, I try to play it cool. "Sounds great! I'm sure I can find the time." I really don't want to miss another date with Tom, especially after the disastrous first date of tonight.

As we walk back to my car, Tom tells me how much he would like to know more about me. I blush and say the same to him as we reach my car. "I could give you a lift home, if you like," I say hopefully.

"It's all good. I only live up the road, and it's a nice night for a walk." He smiles and inches a little closer.

I close my eyes, willing him to kiss me. His lips brush against my cheek and when I open my eyes, he is already walking away. "See you tomorrow night at Luigi's Bistro!" he calls.

Disappointment and electric excitement mingle in my chest. My cheek practically burns where he kissed it, but I so wanted him to snog my face off. "See you tomorrow," I murmur, turning to open my car door.

Then, I spin back in Tom's direction and shout as loud as my voice can handle, "Hey, what time are we having dinner?"

"Eight p.m.!" Tom yells back.

I watch his reflection in my car window until it fades. Then, I get back into my car and drive home. On the way, all I can think about is Tom.

I park my car on the driveway and make my way up to the front door. As I do, a black cat zooms out of the bushes and darts in front of me. I stop in mid-step and gasp. I don't want any bad luck, especially since I have another date with Tom now.

33

I open my front door and close it as softly as I can so as not to wake any of my family. I creep up the stairs like a mouse, tiptoe across the landing, sneak past my parents' bedroom to mine and close my bedroom door. After my ninja adventure, I undress myself for bed, put my phone on the charger and get under the covers.

Tom's face floats in my mind's eye. After a few minutes of lying there, I turn on my front and switch the bedside lamp back on. I sit up and look at the ceiling. Still, all I can do is think about Tom. *What is he doing right now? Is he asleep, dreaming of me?* I want so badly to text him to make sure he got home okay. I reach over and grab my phone to send Tom a goodnight message, being sure to include a kiss emoji. I lay the phone down on my duvet, hoping that I'll receive a reply from Tom soon, but nothing comes.

Just as I put my phone back on my charger, it vibrates and pings. I rush to see if it is from Tom and as I do, I end up dropping my phone down the side of my bed. *Oh fuck!* I reach down to retrieve it and as I am leaning over the side of the mattress, I hit my hand on the back of the bedside table. The jolt of pain makes me yelp, but at least I have the phone in my hand. I open the screen to find a text from my mobile phone provider, telling me how I can save on a promotion they are running. I feel so disappointed.

The time on my phone says 2:00 a.m. I decide to text Lucy—she should be awake at this time on the weekend, because she loves watching all those American talk shows. *Hey, are you awake?* I send her.

There's no reply, so I assume she's skipped the shows today and is already asleep. I reach over to turn off the lamp and begin to drift off to dreamland. My phone vibrates again, startling me from my half-doze. Maybe Lucy was just engrossed in a show and now she wants to talk. I have so much to tell her!

But the text is not from Lucy—it's from Tom! *Hey, thanks for a good night. See you tomorrow!* He ended the text with two kisses. I don't think it was much of a good night, with the bar being so loud and full, and then walking to the other side of town to a pub which turned out to be closed. At least Tom's being nice about it. And he has invited me out on another date!

I text Tom back with, *See you tomorrow*, with two kisses and a smiley face.

I am now excited like a box of Smarties! *How in the world am I going to fall asleep now?* I try to count sheep, but I give up when I reach one hundred. I put both my hands at the back of my head and lie there. It seems like I've only just drifted off when golden light streams through my bedroom window. *It can't be morning already!*

As the sun's rays pour through my curtains, I reach over and look at my phone. Panic floods my body. It is 6 p.m.! I have slept through most of the day! I suppose the excitement of last night required a lot of recovery for my body. Perhaps all the late nights trying to get projects ready for Jessica this week also had something to do with it.

At least the only important thing I have to do today is go on my date with Tom, and I still have two hours to get there. I place my phone back on the table and pull my duvet over my head. As I relax, there is a knock at my bedroom door. I don't say anything. Then, I hear my mum say, "Matt, love, do you have any clothes you need washed?"

"Ugh," I mutter. I am so tired I can barely process what she's saying.

She knocks a little louder and cracks the door open. I drag myself up to a sitting position. "Yes Mum, I have clothes for you. I will bring them down to you in a minute."

"Okay, love," she replies. Her footsteps shuffle away down the hall.

I throw the duvet off and sit on the side of the bed. I pick my phone up and read the text I received from Tom last night, with the two kisses at the end. I can't believe he likes spending time with me!

My mother's voice shouts up the stairs, "Matt, the clothes, love! I am waiting to put the machine on!"

"Coming, Mum!" I quickly throw on the clothes I wore last night and gather my dirty laundry from my basket. It occurs to me that I also need a shirt to wear tonight for my second date with Tom. I place my dirty clothes down on my bed and explore my wardrobe to find something nice. A white shirt, still in its packaging, is stuffed in the back. *This will do nicely*! I pull the shirt out of the plastic wrapping and throw it over my arm as I pick my dirty clothing up off the bed and head downstairs, where my mother is still loading the washing machine.

"Here you go, Mum. My clothes."

"Thank you, Matt!" she replies, taking the pile out of my hands and dumping it in the washing machine—including the shirt I want to wear for my date with Tom tonight!

"Mum! Wait! That's the shirt I'm wearing tonight!" I snatch the shirt out of the washing machine.

"That was lucky, love. I was about to press the start button. How did last night go?"

I give her the run-down, and just as I'm explaining that the Melford Arms was closed, my father enters the kitchen.

"It was probably closed because Tony, the baker, has been popping in and out of their house frequently," Dad says. "Sounds like he's been playing with her baps. You know, the woman who…"

My mother interrupts him. "Oh, I know, the hussy with the oversized breasts. The one whose chest arrives on time and she's fifteen minutes late!"

My dad lets out a laugh and my mother pulls a snide face at him as she continues with the washing. I couldn't care less about the baker's shenanigans—I'm just relieved that my shirt won't be still in the wash when I need it tonight. The white fabric is wrinkled to hell and back, though, so I set the ironing board up and plug the iron in. I smooth the shirt over the board and begin with the sleeve.

A burning smell worms up my nose. I pull the iron away and a brown mark sits on the white fabric. "For fuck's sake, what's this?" I mutter.

I peer at the bottom of the iron. Something brown has melted on its metal plate. "Mum!" I shout.

She rushes over from the other side of the kitchen to see what the matter is; I show her the stain on my shirt and the matching spot on the bottom of the iron.

"Oh, love, this must be Loraine. The iron was fine when I used it this morning, but she used it in the afternoon. She must have gotten something stuck on it."

"Oh well, that's just great. That makes two items of clothing Loraine has ruined for me."

"Calm down, Matt. I will pop next door to see Shirley and ask if she has anything to remove this stain. She bought a new book last week about old wives' remedies for removing stains."

My mother goes next door to see our neighbour, taking my shirt with her. I sit down at the kitchen table and rest my head in my hands. First Mum almost washed my shirt and now Loraine has ruined the sleeve. *Things happen in threes! Two down, one to go.*

My phone vibrates and pings in my trouser pocket. It's a text from Lucy. *Hey, how did your date with sexy Tom go? I want to know all the gory details! Sorry I didn't text back last night.* She ends her message with a kiss emoji, as she always does.

I give her the run-down, which makes my fingers ache from all the typing. Just as I send the text, the back door opens. It's my mother with my shirt.

"There you go love, all sorted for you." She hands me the garment and I check the sleeve. It's snow-white once again.

"Oh, wow! Thanks!" The fabric is still horribly wrinkled, but I don't trust myself to iron it again after what happened last time. "Mum, can you do me another favour?"

"What do you need, love?"

"Would you iron my shirt for me?"

"Yes, of course." She takes my no-longer-stained shirt out of my hand.

I feel a bit guilty about her doing all my chores for me, so I'd better lend a hand. "Hang on, Mum, I'll clean the bottom of the iron for you." I take the iron over to the kitchen sink and use a cloth and some soap to remove the tacky brown lump. What in the world did Loraine stick on there? It looks like some kind of chocolate.

As my mum irons, she restarts the conversation about how my date last night went with Tom. As I tell her about our walk back to the car from the Melford Arms, my phone vibrates and pings. I dash into my trouser pocket to reach it. It's a text from Tom. *Hey, hope you're having a good evening! Looking forward to tonight.* He ends his message with a kiss!

My hands shake as I reply, *Same here.* Oh God, that sounded way too bland.

Mum pauses and says, "Lucy again, love?"

"Yes, Mum." Something about Tom's texts makes me want to keep them all to myself.

Finally, she says, "There you go, love. All ironed for you!"

"Thanks, Mum!" I kiss her on the cheek and she smiles as she proceeds to put the iron and ironing board away for me.

I dash upstairs to the bathroom, hoping no one is in there so I can get ready for tonight. Mercifully, the door is unlocked. *At last, I can have a shower in peace.* I get undressed and jump into the shower. "Owww!" The water is freezing! I forgot to turn the shower on by the cord which heats the water. I leap out to fix my mistake and jump back in with a flash. The water becomes lovely and warm. I could stay in this shower all day and night, but I only allow myself fifteen minutes. I don't want to be late for my dinner date with Tom.

After I brush my teeth, I rub the condensation off the mirror with a towel and rub shaving cream over my face. I take each stroke with the razor carefully. I don't want to cut my face. What will Tom think if I turn up at the restaurant looking like something out of a horror movie?

Dashing to my bedroom, I take out a fresh pair of black boxer shorts and spray deodorant on them so they smell like a summer orchard. Next, I walk over to the mirror and take my time buttoning my shirt up. I don't want to put the buttons in the wrong holes and end up with a lopsided front. After donning my socks and trousers, I walk over to my wall unit and throw a little of the bottle of aftershave on my face. *Not too much this time!* I tell myself. I don't want to make Tom feel like it's an allergy season again.

As I am about to leave my bedroom, my mother calls up the hallway. "Matt, would you like a cuppa?"

I reply, "No, Mum, I am going out now!"

I meet her at the stairs and, once again, she does what all mothers do: fix my clothes to make sure I look smart.

I roll my eyes and chuckle. "Mum, I am not a child. I can dress myself!"

"You'll always be my little boy," she says, standing on her tiptoes and reaching up to pat my head.

I laugh and kiss her on the cheek, and out the door I go to meet Tom. As I get to my car, my phone vibrates with a text from Tom, telling me he has arrived at the restaurant.

I jump into the car and zoom off down the street. Unfortunately, the petrol light flashes. Can I make it to the restaurant without filling up first? Maybe, but I don't want to risk it. And if Tom gets in my car for whatever reason, it could be a bit embarrassing if he sees I'm running low on fuel.

I find the nearest petrol station on the way and fill up the tank. As I am lining up for the counter, I see they sell condoms. I think to myself; *Shall I buy a box? What if we sleep together tonight?*

The queue builds up behind me as my head whirls with indecision. I don't want to lose my place in line—I'm verging on being late as it is—but that means I'll have to ask the fifty-something-year-old sales lady for a box of condoms. As I approach the counter, my hands grow clammy.

"How can I help you?" the lady asks.

I blurt out, "A box of party hats and pump number six for petrol."

She looks at me strangely. "We don't sell party hats. This is a petrol station, not a party shop."

"Oh…okay. Just the petrol, then." I'm not sure whether I'm relieved or dismayed that she didn't know party hats are my personal slang for condoms. As I hand the cash to the sales assistant, my face must be redder than a baboon's bum. I make a quick getaway and I can feel the sales assistant's eyes on me and the customers in the queue shuffle and mutter behind me. I reach the car and open the door, but pause before I get in. Should I go back in and buy the condoms? If I do get the chance to sleep with Tom tonight, what will he think of me if I don't have protection? But I don't think I could face going back in and asking again for a box of condoms from someone who is old enough to be my nan. I decide not to and I drive off.

As I pull up to the restaurant, the clock on my dashboard flicks over to 8 p.m. *Right on time!*

I close my car door and look at the menu board on the wall of the entrance. *Wow! These prices are expensive!* The outside of the restaurant looks posh and, luckily, I don't think I look too out-of-place with my newly ironed shirt. The waiter opens the door for me and Tom waves at me as another waiter leads me to the table.

I have trouble controlling my jaw as I sit down. Tom looks hotter than a piece of chicken cooking on a barbeque, with his top three shirt buttons undone so I can just see the top of his chest, his hair styled to perfection.

"Hey, you found it okay! Not a lot of people do at first." He smiles at me with his perfect teeth.

"Have you been here before, then?"

"No, this is my first time."

"Oh." How does he know that people have trouble finding it if he's never been here before? I'm about to question him, but we are interrupted by the waiter bringing us over the menus and asking us what we would like to drink. I order a pint of lager and Tom orders the same.

Tom studies the menu with his eyebrows drawn slightly together and his lips pursed in concentration. I just can't take my eyes off him. He looks up, his blue eyes piercing mine. "Matt, what do you fancy?"

"You," I say.

He laughs. "I think I will order garlic mushrooms and spaghetti carbonara. There's plenty of time to order dessert later."

"Oh, I hope so," I mutter. I force myself to look at the menu, but all I really want is to get Tom into bed.

The waiter returns with our drinks, placing Tom's down first and then mine. "Are we ready to order?"

Tom smiles. "Yes. Matt, you go first."

"No, you first." I tear my eyes away from Tom and try to spear the words on the menu with my gaze. I just need a little more time to actually figure out what options there are. Why does Tom have to distract me so much?

"I'll have the garlic mushrooms and spaghetti…actually, no, on second thoughts, I'll have the steak." Tom nods and hands his menu back to the waiter.

"And for you, sir?" the waiter says, turning to me.

"Uh…I'll have the same." I mentally kick myself as the waiter takes my menu. That steak is bloody expensive.

Tom starts the conversation by saying, "So you're a red meat kind of guy, eh?"

"I love any kind of meat."

He bows his head and starts to giggle. "Oh, you do, do you?"

Is Tom flirting with me? My mind freezes. I have no idea what to say.

Tom says, "What's that aftershave you're wearing? It smells good."

Okay. Aftershave. Focus, Matt. "Oh, it's The One by that famous footballer…aww, I can't remember his name."

"Cool," Tom says.

Well, that line of conversation went nowhere. I search my brain for some more interesting topics, but then my phone vibrates. I put my hand in my pocket out of habit, then pull out my phone. It would be rude to text on a date.

A riff of music blasts from Tom's pocket and he pulls his own phone out to look at the screen. "Would you excuse me, Matt? I am just off for a ciggy." He stands up and walks off with his still-ringing phone in one hand and his cigarettes in other.

I'm momentarily taken aback—he ditched me to answer his phone!—but I decide to give him the benefit of the doubt.

It must be an important call. I take advantage of his absence by reading the text I just received. It's from Lucy, asking how my night is going.

It's going well, I write back. *Now piss off.* I add a kiss and laughing emoji.

The waiter brings our starters to the table, but Tom has not returned. "He'll be back soon," I say to the waiter. The waiter nods and sets Tom's food down at the vacant place.

Twenty minutes later, I find myself wondering if he is okay. I would have thought he'd take care of his business as quickly as possible if he's on a date and there's delicious food to be eaten. I begin to nibble at my starter, but my worry quenches my appetite. *I'd better see if he is okay.* Or worse—if he's ditched me. I put my fork down, but just as I am about to head off to look for Tom, he appears from the toilet.

He sits back in his chair with no apology or explanation of what took him so long. "Is the food good?"

I say, "Yeah, it's delicious."

He takes a mouthful of his. "Mmm, you're right! This is really good!"

The main courses arrive in short order. Tom takes a bite and accidentally smears some sauce on the side of his mouth. "How's the steak?" he asks after swallowing.

I can't help laughing and Tom smiles. "What's so funny?"

"You have a little sauce on the side of your face."

He tries to dab it away, but he just ends up spreading it around. I dip a serviette in some water and lend him a hand. His lips are so good-looking—I just want to kiss him. "There you go, it's gone," I say, a tad breathlessly.

We finish our main meal, and the waiter returns with the dessert menus. He lingers as we look at the choices, but truth be told, I'm not focusing on food with the delicious hunk of man sitting across from me.

"Could we have a bit more time?" I ask.

The waiter says, "Sure," and leaves.

Despite how nervous Tom makes me, I can't resist any longer. I remove my shoe and move my leg up to where Tom is sitting. I slowly glide my foot over Tom's leg and move it down to his groin area, rubbing my foot over his penis—which I am pleased to find fully erected in his trousers.

He grins at me. "Boy, it's starting to get hot in here."

I move my foot closer to his zipper, gaining confidence. He likes me! My own crotch is getting quite hot and bothered too.

Tom giggles. "Stop. You're turning me on."

"You're the one turning me on."

"Oh, really?"

"Oh, yes."

"Shall we have dessert elsewhere?"

Finally! "I thought you were never going to ask." I laugh, rubbing my foot over his penis again.

Just then, the waiter returns. Tom quickly removes my foot from his groin area and I end up banging my leg on the table. Pain rips through my shin. "Fuck," I say through clenched teeth.

"Are you all right, sir?" the waiter asks.

"Yes," I say weakly.

Tom tells the waiter we are going to skip dessert, which is music to my ears, and asks for the bill. I am so turned on and I know Tom is too. Tom excuses himself from the table.

A smile stretches across my face. He is off to buy the party hats!

The waiter returns with the bill and my heart sinks as I take in the cost. I root around in my wallet, but my card is absent. I panic for a second before I remember that I removed my card a couple of days ago in order to put my details into an online shopping app. It's probably still sitting on my dresser. But I only have thirty pounds in cash, and the steak I ate costs far more than that.

What I am going to do now? I can't expect Tom to pay for the meal!

A few moments after Tom returns, he looks at the bill and says, "Hey Matt, this is my treat."

"No, let me pay mine," I say, though I don't know how I'll do it. I suppose I could call my mum and ask her to bring my card to the restaurant. How embarrassing.

"Don't worry about it. You only live once." Tom pays the bill against my protests, though I'm secretly relieved. We leave the restaurant and excitement builds up inside me. *It's happening!*

Tom asks, "What do you want to do now?"

"You know exactly what," I say.

We find an empty doorway a few buildings down from the restaurant and we can't resist one another anymore. We start kissing and my hand slides down his body to the erection in his underwear. I rub him as our tongues dance together.

He whispers in my ear, "I want you so bad."

"I want you too," I breathe.

"Can I come back to your place?" Tom says, and kisses my neck.

"Uh...no. No, we can't go there. There's, um, decorators at work." It's such an unconvincing excuse, but there's no way we can do what we want to do with my parents and sister around. "Can we go to your place?"

"No," he mumbles into my neck, "but I do know where we can go. I have my keys with me, if you don't mind going to the Coffee House."

"I will go anywhere with you. I want you so bad."

We quickly dash to the car and head to the Coffee House. I drive with one hand on the steering wheel and the other on Tom's groin. We arrive at the Coffee House, he opens the front door and the alarm goes off. He quickly disables it and grabs my hand. "Come on!"

Where are we going? He takes us to the back of the Coffee House and moves two tables and some chairs. I begin to unbutton my shirt as he comes back to me. Our bodies align as one. I start to undress him.

"Have you got any party hats...I mean, rubbers?" I stutter.

He pulls one out of his wallet. "Party hats aplenty."

"I'm a virgin," I blurt.

This seems to excite him even more. Half-naked, we cannot keep our hands off of each other. I glide my hands down his abdomen and passionately kiss his neck. I undo his belt as he unfastens my button and zipper. His erection bulges as I caress it through his underwear, and a rush goes through my body. I slowly pull away from him, dropping to my knees. I stare up at him as I pull the zip down on his trousers. He practically leaps out of them. I stand back up and start to kiss down his body as he pulls my own trousers down. His nipples become solid as a rock under my mouth. His manhood is now bursting to be released in his white boxer shorts.

He takes his boxers off. "Lie down on the sofa."

I obey. His commands turn me on. He lies on top of me and kisses me passionately.

"I want you so much," I moan into his ear.

With that, he sits up and grabs the condom. He removes it from its wrapper and wets the end. "It might hurt. But I'll try to be gentle."

I just lie there and let him take control. He makes love to me, and it feels so amazing. Afterwards, we kiss for what must be thirty minutes.

I giggle as the absurdity of the situation hits me. I just lost my virginity to a gorgeous man on the sofa in a coffee shop. "Thank you," I say.

"How was I?" he asks.

"It was perfect."

He kisses me one more time, taps my leg and says, "We better move."

I wish I could lie there for the rest of the night with him, but he jumps off the sofa and gets dressed in subdued lighting. I have the most beautiful view of his fit body and his manhood.

Did that really happen, or was I just dreaming?

"Get dressed. I'm going to go for a ciggy. You better get rid of the evidence." He grins at me.

I jump off the sofa to get dressed. Even after we are both clothed, we can't seem to keep our hands off one another. As he pulls up his trousers, I push them down while kissing him passionately. I touch his boxer shorts to pull them down and he shifts away. "Easy, tiger!"

I take the hint and back off. "Where's the toilet?" I ask as I am buttoning my shirt. He points me in the right direction.

When I get into the cubicle, I take my phone out of my trouser pocket. Thank God I didn't crack the screen during that hot steamy lovemaking. I text Lucy, *Guess what's just happened!*

A minute later, my phone rings. Lucy says, "You'd better tell me everything right this second."

"I just had sex with Tom in the coffee shop!" My voice squeaks with glee. Somehow, saying it out loud makes it even more real.

"No way! You're kidding me!" She gasps.

"No, honestly!"

I hear Tom coming towards the door, so I hang up on Lucy. It would be so embarrassing if he caught me discussing what just happened with my best friend. The door cracks open. "You okay?" Tom asks.

I open the door all the way and throw myself at him and we are kissing again. After a few minutes, Tom pulls away. "We better get out of here, just in case someone sees us. And I need a fag."

As we leave, I look over at the sofa where we just made love. All the tables and chairs are back in place, as if nothing ever happened. But the memory of Tom making hot, passionate love to me, taking my virginity away from me in the heat of desire, remains imprinted in my mind. Or was that all just a dream?

Tom asks me to wait outside while he sets the alarms. I watch him through the glass window of the door and instead of setting the alarms, fiddles with his phone. I wish he'd hurry up—it's freezing out here. A few moments later, Tom goes to the alarm box and does his thing, then joins me and locks the coffee shop door. As we walk away, Tom lights up a ciggy and says, "I need this."

We pass a war memorial bench, where I sit while he finishes his cigarette. Once he stubs it out and tosses it in a nearby bin, we start to talk about life in general. After a couple of minutes of conversation, we start to kiss again. I don't care who sees us. I just want to snog his face off.

Suddenly, I hear footsteps coming toward us, accompanied by the sound of male voices. Tom pushes me away quickly and whips his phone out of his pocket to stare intently at the screen. I do the same. My heart pounds. I feel like a secret agent in one of those action films.

One of the men in the group pauses next to us. "Oi," he says. "Got a light?"

"Yes." Tom hands his lighter to the guy.

The man grunts and lights a ciggy. "So what are you two up to, then?"

I shrug. "Sitting on a bench."

"Hey, Mike!" one of the man's friends calls. "Stop yakking and let's go!"

"Thanks for the light," the man says and walks off to join the rest of his mates.

Tom smiles. "That was a close one. I thought we were going to get caught." He lets out a little giggle.

I move closer to Tom and wrap my arms around him. We kiss again; my hand is on his knee and I am heading towards his groin again, when we hear a noise behind us. Tom stops and pushes me away again. We wait a few moments and the noise is gone.

Tom says, "We better make a move."

"Just one more kiss?"

He says, "Yeah, sure, but let's start walking." He plants one on me quickly.

We take a shortcut through the park to get back to my car, just in case we see the group of guys again. As we speed-walk past the trees and flowerbeds, Tom asks me about my family. He tells me that he is an only child.

"What is your family name?" I ask. It's so odd that I've had sex with him and I don't even know his surname.

"It's Sheppard. What's yours?"

"Storm," I reply.

"That's a pretty cool name. I live with my father. My mother ran off with the local baker," he shudders, as if reliving a bad memory. I remember Dad telling me and Mum about the landlady running off with a man from the Melford Arms. Could that be where Tom lives? I shouldn't push it further, though—I might upset him. I change the subject to enquire about his work schedule.

We reach the exit to the park and I just can't resist the temptation. I push Tom up against a tree and we kiss. I can see and feel Tom getting turned on.

"We should go behind the bushes," he groans.

"It's dark and I can't see," I stammer.

"Then use the light on my phone."

Before we know it, we are in the wooded part of the park. I start to undo his shirt and he stops me, moving my hand down to his trousers. He puts his hand on my bum and squeezes it firmly. My skin blazes all over. Despite the cold air, I might as well be walking through fire. He undoes the button on my trousers and pulls them down with my boxer shorts. "Bend over against the tree," he commands as he opens his wallet to take out another condom.

He makes love to me until he climaxes for the second time in a night. It didn't seem as long as the first time. I feel his lips on my neck. "You have a great ass," he whispers.

I turn around and start kissing him again until he pulls away. "We have to start going home before it gets too late. I need a shower," he says.

"I need a shower too," I say as we both get dressed.

He lights up a cigarette as we head back through the bushes and trees to the main path of the park. I grab his hand. "Wow, I can't believe I had sex twice in one night on the first go."

Tom giggles. "How was it for you?"

"It was amazing and I feel horny again."

As we are about to reach the park exit, I think, *I need to tell him I am falling in love with him.* I just need the right moment. No—fuck it. There's no time like the present. I stop Tom and move in front of him as he finishes his ciggy. I take both of his hands. "I need to tell you something."

His deep blue eyes are like twin lakes. "What, Matt?"

I take a deep breath. "I am falling in love with you."

There's silence. Tom releases my hand from his. My stomach sinks down to my feet. Why did I say that? He must think I'm so clingy and naïve.

Finally, Tom opens his mouth to reply, but a guy passes and looks at us. Tom says, "Well, I guess this is where we say goodnight."

"Can I give you a lift?" Maybe if we spend more time together on the drive home, he'll say whatever he was planning on saying.

"No, that's okay. I'll walk."

We kiss, but there's no tongue, and I wrap my arms around Tom. As I do, I can see a shadow of a figure a few yards up the path.

"Can I see you again?" I ask.

"Sure. I will send you a text."

Well, I suppose it's a good sign that he's not breaking up with me right now. I walk out of the park, but I take a sneaky look back to see Tom running up the path. Odd.

I open my car door and sit inside, but don't drive off straight away. I reach inside my pocket and grab my phone to text Lucy. *I'm in love. Tell you all about it later.*

As I put my seatbelt on, ready to drive off, my phone rings. "I want to know everything!" Lucy says in my ear.

"Meet me at Rosie's Cafe in the morning," I say.

On the way home, my phone vibrates and I pull over. It could just be Lucy whining about being kept in suspense, but it could also be the promised text from the man I just confessed love to.

My breath hitches as I see Tom's name on the screen. I open the message.

I'm falling in love with you, too. Can I see you tomorrow night?

He ends his text message with four kisses. All my apprehension evaporates into one huge explosion of joy. Christmas has come early this year! And my present is true love!

Chapter Three

The next day, my mother knocks at my bedroom door as per usual. "Matt, love, do you have any dirty clothes? I am putting the machine on in five!"

I get dressed in my jumper and jeans, grab my dirty clothes and open the door to face my mum. Tom's aftershave still lingers on the shirt I wore last night, which sits at the top of the pile. The smell begins to turn me on and it's only 9 a.m.

"There you go, Mum!" I hand the clothes to her.

She looks at the shirt. "What's this, Matt? You seem to have a green stain on it."

An image of Tom making love to me in the park flashes into my mind. "Do I?" I say, trying to sound nonchalant.

She looks at me with a puzzled face and I make my way down the stairs. As I reach the bottom, I grab my phone from my jacket and text Lucy to tell her I am on my way to Rosie's Café.

My mother's voice drifts down from the top of the stairs as she talks to my dad. "You know, dear, I just don't understand it. The shirt was squeaky clean yesterday and now there's a green stain right there. It's like he's been rolling around on the lawn or something."

It seems this mystery is the topic of the hour this Sunday morning. But there's no time to think of an excuse—I have to get to the café. "Bye, Mum and Dad, and Sis!" I shout.

My mother calls, "Matt, where are you off to now? You hardly spend any time at home these days."

"Busy life, Mum!" I reply, shutting the front door behind me. I debate taking the car to Rosie's Café, but it is just two streets away from my house, so I decide to walk there. It's a lovely day. On the way, I cast my mind back to last night and how wonderful it was, and even more so now that Tom has told me he loves me.

My phone vibrates; it's a message from Lucy, telling me she is running late.

I arrive at the café and find a table in the window so that Lucy will see me when she arrives. Before I can even sit my bum down on the seat, the waitress pounces on me like a jaguar. "And what can I get you today, sir?"

"I have just arrived. Give me five minutes."

"Very well, sir." She bustles away to serve the next table. I take my phone out of my jacket just to have a look at Facebook, when I receive another text from Lucy saying she has arrived and is trying to find a parking space. I text back, *It's a Sunday, there are plenty of parking spaces, lol.*

Found one, she replies a few moments later. *Just touching up my makeup.*

It's not London fashion week, it's just a backstreet café. I add a smile and a kiss.

The waitress returns to take my order and I ask for two milky coffees.

"Do you mean lattes, sir?"

"That's the one, yes."

"D'you want to order any food?"

"No, just the coffees for now."

She leaves just as Lucy walks in through the door. My friend's face glows with the amount of cosmetics she's wearing.

"You got more make-up on you than Coco the clown!" I say with a grin.

She laughs. "At least I look fabulous." She hits me gently with her bag, places her coat on the back of the chair and sits down. "So, come on. Tell me all about it!"

The waitress arrives with our coffee to us. I say to Lucy, "I ordered you a milky coffee. I mean…a latte."

"With skimmed milk?" Lucy asks.

"Um…I just asked for two milky coffees." I turn to the waitress. "Do you know if the milk is skimmed?"

She laughs. "How the frig would I know? Milk is milk!" She walks off.

Lucy stares at her retreating figure. "How rude!" She takes a sip of her drink. "Hmm, it's quite creamy. Probably semi-skimmed."

"I'm sorry, Lucy. I should've waited to order till you arrived."

She flaps a hand. "Never mind. Thank you, Matt." She sits forward in her chair. "Now, spill!"

I grab Lucy's hand. "I am in love with the most gorgeous man on the planet. He is fit as fuck and the sex was amazing! He made love to me twice!"

Lucy's eyes grow round. "Wow, twice in one night! Where did you do it?" She takes a sip of coffee.

"The first time was on the sofa at the back of the coffee shop." I could swear I already told Lucy about that, but maybe she didn't believe me and wanted to see if she could catch me out by asking me again. Well, you can't trip me up that easily, Lucy. Doubt me all you want—my magical first time was as real as can be.

Lucy splutters coffee out of her mouth and she bursts into laughter. "You had sex on the sofas in the coffee shop?"

"Well, not all the sofas. Just the one by the table and chairs."

Lucy giggles. "Next time we go there, be sure to point it out to me so I know not to sit there." She dabs at the spilled coffee with a napkin. "You said that was the first time. What about the second?"

I pause for suspense. I haven't had any good romantic gossip to spill in ages, and I intend to milk this for all it's worth. "In the park. Well, in the woodland, behind the bushes."

Lucy covers her mouth. "No way!"

"Yes way," I grin.

"Did you use protection?"

"Of course, Mum."

"No, Matt, you have to be so careful in this day and age. Some guys don't care. They just want to have sex with no protection."

"Well, Tom is not like other men. He had condoms in his wallet ready. Oh, speaking of condoms…" I tell her the story of my party hat mishap at the petrol station, which leads to me giving her all the details about the night, including how Tom ended up paying for my steak dinner.

Lucy laughs. "You did well. A meal and two shags in one night!"

I puff out my chest. "You know me. I always come up smelling of roses!"

"You're not wrong! When are you seeing Tom again?"

"Tonight, Lucy!" A buzz of excitement goes through me just thinking about it.

"When do I get to meet him?"

"Soon!" I say.

I explain to Lucy how I confessed my love to Tom and he reciprocated. I'm crazy about him. I can't eat and I can't sleep. I just want to be with him night and day.

"I am so happy for you, Matt. I can't even get a man. God knows I have tried many. Even those that are married or living with their parents!" She pulls a face.

I giggle. "Don't worry, hun. Mr Right is out there for us all."

"You're only saying that because you have fallen in love with your Mr Loverman Tom." She grins slyly. "What's he like under his clothes?"

"Oh, he's bloody amazing!" I melt like an ice-cream on a summer's day explaining how fit he is.

"Does he have a big one?"

"Oh, yes, there are no problems. When he was born, he was truly blessed." We both burst out in a giggle fit. Lucy wants to know more about Tom's body parts, but we are interrupted by the waitress, who rudely tells us they are closed with a sour expression on her face. I glance at the clock—Rosie's does close early on Sundays, but you'd have thought they'd be a bit nicer about it.

When we exit the café, I say, "Does that waitress remind you of someone?"

"Hmm." Lucy taps her chin. "I think I need a clue."

"She has the loudest gob in Kelford, she wears bargain boxed shoes, and we will be seeing her tomorrow!"

"Could it be…the Wicked Witch Jessica?" Lucy wiggles her fingers in an impression of witchy talons.

"That's the one," I snicker. "Come on, I will walk you back to your car."

As we head towards the car park, my phone vibrates. I don't answer it—it's not going to be from my Tom.

Lucy says to me, "Are you going to read your text?"

"No point. It will probably be one of those PPI companies. You know, they sent me a text the other day informing me I have a claim. I don't think so! I don't even have PPI!"

"But you never know. It might be from someone important."

I love Lucy to bits, but she is getting on my nerves today! She probably thinks the text is from Tom and wants to get the gossip first-hand. I open the screen on my phone and it's a text from my mother, asking if I can pop into Mr Petal's convenience store on the way home to pick up a bag of potatoes and a bar of chocolate with the bubbles and mint in it.

Lucy peers over my shoulder. "I shall give you a lift."

"Oh hun, it's out of your way. You live on the other end of town."

Lucy does not take no for an answer and before I know it, I am in the passenger seat of her car. Oh well, might as well make the best of it. "What kind of sounds do you have?" I ask.

"Oh, the usual. Show stopper music." She laughs and just as she goes to turn on the CD player, my phone rings. My stomach flips as I read the name displayed on the screen. Tom is calling me.

I accept the call and speak in a soft voice. "Hello, you sexy beast."

Lucy lets out a quiet squeal. On the phone, Tom giggles. "Why are you whispering?"

"Is that Loverman Tom?" Lucy says at the top of her voice.

I feel like I could just die on the spot. I give Lucy a nudge, hoping she gets the message to *shut up*.

"Oh, sorry," she giggles.

"I'm sorry, Tom," I say. "Don't worry. She is going back into her box."

Tom chuckles. "She seems fun."

I begin to tell Tom how wonderful last night was, but Lucy keeps glancing at me, trying to earwig in on my conversation. "Tom, hold on one moment." I say as I put the phone down and turn to Lucy. "Keep your eyes on the road and concentrate, hun! You nearly knocked one of those traffic cones over!"

"They shouldn't be on the road!" she tries to defend herself.

"That's what they are used for!" I exclaim. Tom's laughter crackles from the phone speaker. I lift it back to my ear. "Again, sorry about Lucy. But yes, last night was amazing."

"Was I really that good?" he says.

"Well, you have a tool and you know how to use it. Honestly, I am horny right now just thinking about it."

"You flatter me," Tom says. "Anyway, the reason I'm calling you is because the Under-The-Rainbow club is shutting down and we've been invited to the closing party. Do you fancy it? Bring Louise with you, too."

"Her name is Lucy. And are you sure? You know she's as mad as a box of frogs!"

Lucy slams on the brakes and I almost hit the dashboard. "Hey, what'd you do that for?" I laugh.

Tom says, "What happened?"

"Oh, Lucy just decided to pull a James Bond driver stunt," I say. Lucy shoots me a snide look.

"Sounds fun. So, are you up for tonight?" Tom presses.

"Yes, but I won't be able to stay out really late, because Lucy and I have to work early in the morning."

Lucy leans towards the phone and shouts, "Don't worry, Tom! I will be there!"

I push Lucy away from the phone. Tom says, "Make sure you bring her. I think she could be interesting company."

"You can say that again!" I wink at Lucy.

"I shall meet you both there, then."

"Sounds good. I love you."

"I love you too," he says.

My heart floats like a balloon. "Tom, I want you so bad."

"You will have me tonight," he reassures me.

"See you tonight, then." I smile to myself. We say I love you one last time together and I blow a kiss into the phone before hanging up.

"Why have we stopped, Lucy?" I say.

"Um…" She gestures out the window. It appears we have arrived at Petal's and I didn't even notice.

"Are you coming in?" I ask her.

"No, I am getting ready for my threesome." She grins wryly.

"You really are crazier than a box of frogs!" I giggle. Lucy gives me a slight tap on my face. I get out of the car and say, "Thanks for the lift! I shall see you tonight."

As I walk into Petal's, Lucy rolls down the passenger window and shouts, "You never give me kisses like the one you gave to Tom on the phone!"

I run back and give Lucy a kiss on the cheek.

"There you go!" she says. "Now, what do you think I should wear tonight?"

"Something that stands out!" Though she'll have a hard time standing out among all the fabulous flamboyant people who frequent Under-The-Rainbow.

"We can go into the club together. I will meet you by the clock tower," she says as she pulls off.

I wave after her, then turn and enter the shop. Mr Petal sits behind his counter, talking to someone on his phone, just like he is every time I come here. He smiles at me and angles the phone's mouthpiece away from his face. "Do you need any help?"

"No, thank you Mr Petal." Under my breath, I add, "Stay on your phone." As I make my way to the vegetable section, I pass the magazine stand. A cover with a fit guy on it catches my gaze. I close my eyes for a second, thinking of my Tom showing off his six-pack body with his matching huge package. Luckily, it won't be long before I see him again. I grab all of the items my mum needs and pay Mr Petal, who manages to complete the transaction while still talking on the phone.

I arrive home and place the groceries on the kitchen table. "Thanks, love," my mum says, kissing me on the cheek. "Can I settle up with you when I get paid?"

"Yes, of course." As I help her put the potatoes away, I add, "Oh, Mum, I forgot to tell you that I am going out again tonight." This will make three days in a row—the whole weekend—that I've spent the night out.

Her mouth tightens a little bit, but all she says is, "Don't forget you've got work tomorrow."

"Yes, Mum." I leave the kitchen and walk upstairs to my bedroom to start selecting my outfit for tonight.

A few hours later, my mum calls out from the bottom of the stairs, "Matt, your dinner is ready!"

I throw on the clothes I picked out, spray on some aftershave and I am ready to hit the town. I dance my way down the stairs, just singing some random song which comes into my head. Mum's Sunday roast dinner is delicious, but I down it as fast as I can and dart out the door like a bolt of lightning. As I reach the end of the driveway, I realise I forgot to kiss my mother on the cheek like I usually do. Oh well.

Car or bus? Bus it is! As I walk to the bus stop, I buzz with excitement at the thought of seeing Tom for the third night in a row. My weekend has been an amazing one and I don't want it to end; but Monday is just around the corner and then it's back to five days in prison.

It's not long before the bus arrives. I buy a single ticket to take me to the stop next to the clock tower. Nestling down on a blue-carpeted seat, I text Lucy to tell her that I am on the way. It seems to take forever for the rattling vehicle to get from one end of the town to the other.

The bus heaves with people. Next to me, a young man whines into his phone, grumbling about how shit life is. A few rows down, a man with a cardboard sign yells, "Judgment day is not too far away! Repent before it is too late!" Another passenger bops along to the music on his headphones, singing a very out-of-tune version of a popular Top 40 song. A smelly guy sits beside me, and the memory of that time I was stuck in the lift surrounded by BO flashes into my head. I press my nose into my sleeve to dilute the walking odour sitting next to me. I wish the bus would hurry up and arrive so I can be free.

The bus arrives at my stop and I leap out of my seat like a jumping bean to be the first at the doors.

Finally, I step off the bus and run straight into Lucy, who is dolled up to the nines with red lipstick and a lovely dress that suits her perfectly.

I nod approvingly. "Did you just get off of the red carpet?"

She giggles. "I just wanted to look my best for our threesome with Tom."

"Uh...threesome?"

"Yeah, that's what all you men want, isn't it?" She laughs. "Don't worry, I'm only joking."

I laugh and lead her to the Under-The-Rainbow club. Tom loiters outside, smoking a ciggy and talking to two other guys.

Lucy taps me and says, "There's your Prince Charming! Who are his friends?"

"I'll tell you when I meet them in about two seconds." I stride towards Tom with a huge smile stretching across my face, Lucy at my side.

Tom stubs out his ciggy and beams at me. "Ah, there you are! Dan and Paul, this is Matt. Matt, meet Dan and Paul."

My happiness falters a little bit. I would have thought that, after confessing our love for each other, Tom might introduce me as his boyfriend or partner, instead of just 'Matt'. Lucy and I exchange a glance and judging by her drawn-together eyebrows, she's probably thinking the same thing.

I brush off my misgivings. Maybe Tom already explained our relationship status to them. "Hi, I am Matt," I say, shaking Dan's and Paul's hands.

"Yes, Tom just said your name," Dan says.

"Oh." My face grows warm. I smooth things over by introducing Lucy to Tom, Dan and Paul. She grins at them and twirls a strand of perfectly styled hair around her finger.

I whisper to her, "You got no chance. They are on my bus."

"Well, anyone can change buses. Especially when it gets crowded, if you know what I mean." She winks at me.

I just shake my head and chuckle to myself. As we stand and talk, a lesbian winks at Lucy, making her turn bright red.

"Hey, Lucy, you have pulled!" I say.

She nudges me and mutters, "I don't drink from the furry cup, Matt. As you know, I like cock, and lots of it."

"Yeah, when you can get it, that is," I chuckle.

Tom says, "It's getting cold. Shall we head on in?"

Oh, Tom, you won't be cold later on! I think to myself. As we walk through the doors, I tap Tom's bum. Dan and Paul are talking to Lucy, which gives me the perfect opportunity to whisper to Tom, "Come on, give me a kiss." He raises an eyebrow and obliges.

Dan and Paul lead us over to the VIP area of the club, which has been reserved for us all. I have to work hard to prevent my jaw from dangling open. "Is this really for us?"

"It's not what you know, babe, it's who you know," Tom whispers in my ear. OMG, did Tom really just call me his babe? I could get used to that.

We sit at the table and Lucy pushes me closer to Tom. I push her the other way and she knocks into a passing bartender who was bringing us glasses of champagne. Lucy ends up in a perfumed heap on the floor and no one can control their laughter, including her. We pull her back up off the floor onto the seating area and I apologise for making her take a tumble.

"That was lucky," Dan says as the bartender straightens up and passes out our drinks. "None of the glasses fell off the tray."

I say, "Aw, don't worry. Even if they did spill, we could have gotten down on our hands and knees with straws to suck it up."

Tom and Lucy giggle, but Dan and Paul just sip their champagne and look at each other with impassive faces.

I say to Tom, "It's a shame that this place is closing. It has a cool atmosphere."

"Oh, it's not closing completely down," Dan says. "Paul and I have bought the lease. We are going to be closing for a week, changing the name and springing back open like a jack-in-the-box."

My eyes widen. Dan and Paul seem to be living the dream. What could be cooler than owning your own nightclub? Well, owning a toyshop, maybe.

"Cor!" Lucy says. "So what will the new name be?"

Before Dan can reply, the resident drag princess, Polly Easylay, sashays up to our table.

"Here she is," Paul says.

Polly says, "Excuse me! I'm a dame, darling." She runs a long pink fingernail over Tom's cheek. "Mmm, looks like my supper has arrived."

Dan, Paul and Tom giggle and I join in a tad awkwardly, but Lucy folds her arms and presses her mouth into a thin line.

"Does he have a well-packed lunch box?" Polly asks me, putting her hand on Tom's crotch.

"Uh…" I open and shut my mouth a few times. I don't know whether to laugh, or to tell her off for touching my Tom's penis.

Tom laughs. "You can rub it all you like, but it's not going to stand to attention for you."

Polly replies, "Oh, I think that means you need Viagra, love."

Dan and Paul laugh, but I snicker quietly to myself. I know just how amazing Tom's penis is.

Lucy stands up and shoves Polly away from Tom. "What do you think you're doing?"

Dan says, "Let's calm down, ladies. This is a respectable establishment."

Lucy pulls a face at Polly, and the princess snorts. "Back off. Drag is my armour, darling, no matter how you look at it. Once I become Bambi, nobody can hurt me. Not you in your mother-handed-down clothes, nor any of the drunk assholes in this club."

Fuming from Polly's viper tongue, Lucy leaps from her seat and throws the glass of bubbly into Polly's face.

The two women stood there frozen for a few moments, as if they were hypnotised. The bubbly trickles down Polly's face and her beautiful makeup starts to run like if an artist had tipped their water over onto a painting. When the first drop of liquid slides off her chin and onto her chest, Polly begins to shout.

"You bitch!" she screams. "Look what you have done! This dress cost over *five hundred pounds*—that's a damn sight—more than your mother's hand-me-downs, you old troll!"

Fear flits across Lucy's face, but then she begins to giggle, a high-pitched sound full of hysteria and victory. I join in, the laughter releasing the tension from my chest, and Tom, Dan and Paul follow suit a few seconds later.

Polly snarls and raises her fist to hit Lucy across the face. Lucy ducks out of the way and shoves her hands into Polly's torso. The drag queen loses her balance and falls into the nearby table, her wig falling off her head and floating down to land in a neat pile on the floor.

A roar of laughter erupts from the nearby crowd and I have to hold my sides to stop myself from splitting in two with hilarity. A wigless Polly stands up, composes herself and goes to take another swipe at Lucy, but Dan and Paul grab her arms. "All right," Paul says, "that's quite enough."

Lucy sniffs, wipes her nose and lunges at Polly without warning. Tom and I stop Lucy by pushing her back down in her seat.

Lucy doesn't seem fazed, though her makeup is smudged under her eyes. "Enjoy your fall, Polly," she says with a snigger.

I keep my grip firmly on her shoulder in case she tries to make a break for it again. "Enough, Lucy. You're going to get us thrown out." I take a deep breath and bite my lip to avoid laughing again—I don't want to encourage Lucy, no matter how funny the scene was.

Paul says, "Polly, love, go and dry yourself off and fix your makeup. You're on in five."

"But my dress is ruined!" Polly stares down at the discoloured trail the bubbly left all down her chest.

"Well, change into something different, then. But be quick!"

As Polly begins to head toward the dressing room, Tom says, "I need a ciggy after that warm-up act. You coming, Dan?"

Polly throws a scoff over her shoulder.

As they are about to leave the table, Polly says, "Oh, off for a shag, are we? I shall see you out there." She walks behind them, giving Lucy an evil look and a grin.

Lucy puts her two fingers up at the retreating Polly and says to me, "I don't like her. What sort of name is Bambi, anyway?"

I try to explain, but I give up halfway through. Paul clears his throat and begins to explain their plans for the club. Lucy takes some audible deep breaths and asks again what they are renaming the club.

Tom and Dan return to the table with cocktails for us all, and Dan says, "Let's raise a toast to our new club, BillyJeans!"

"To BillyJeans!" we all chorus, clinking our glasses.

Lucy takes a sip of her cocktail just as a new song comes on over the speakers. "Oh, this is my favourite!" She leaps to her feet and runs to the dance floor.

Dan and Paul are kissing one and another and I move around to Tom, running my hand up his leg and kissing him slowly. I'm just starting to undo his shirt when Lucy comes back to the table. "That's my week's worth of exercise!" she says as I pull back from Tom.

I'm just about to make a joke about my own version of exercise when a familiar figure catches my eye. Lewis, the post guy from work, is perched on a stool at the corner of the bar.

I gently kick Lucy, who seems to be lost in something on her phone. "Lucy, is that Lewis from work?"

She looks up and squints in the direction I point. "Oh, fuck, it is," she says.

"I thought it was. I never knew he was gay."

"Neither did I," she says as she sucks on the straw of her cocktail. "Well, we don't know for sure that he doesn't like women. This might be your chance to get some cock tonight. You know what they say—everything comes to those who wait, and tonight is your turn, hun."

"Piss off, Matt," she mumbles into her drink. Tom, Dan, Paul, and I burst into laughter, and Lucy puts her middle finger up at us.

"Who is Lewis?" Tom asks.

I explain it to him and at that moment, Lewis slides off his stool and walks past our table.

Lucy shouts, "Hi Lewis!" I groan inwardly. You goby-cow, Lucy! Now we are going to be stuck with Lewis all night!

Lewis pauses. "Oh, hi, Lucy. Matt."

"I never knew you were gay!" Lucy blurts.

I glance at Lucy and pull a face. Lewis says, "That's because I'm not. You look so different out of your work clothes."

Lucy says, "If you're not gay, then why are you in here?"

I poke her. "You don't have to be gay to visit a gay club. Obviously. I mean, you're here." Tom and Lewis laugh, and Lewis tells us all he just likes to come here because of all the hen parties.

"Now you know why he is not gay," I say.

"Oh, shut your face." Lucy slaps my hand and turns to Lewis. "Come on, I'm bored of third-wheeling. Let's dance." Before Lewis can say anything, Lucy whisks him off to the dancefloor.

I say to Tom, "Alone, at last." He sips his cocktail, leans over and kisses me. I feel as if I am melting like those ice cubes in our drinks. Time seems to stop as I lose myself in him.

Tom pulls back and looks over my shoulder. "Well, the privacy was good while it lasted."

"Huh?" I turn to see Lucy and Lewis coming back to the table together, hand-in-hand. I smirk at Lucy. "Oh, yeah? What's going on here?"

Lucy blushes. "Um..." She glances at Lewis, who is all smiles.

Tom looks at his phone. "Hey, did you know it's almost 3:30 a.m.?"

My eyes go wide. "3:30 a.m.! Shit, we'd better go, Lucy. We have work in the morning. You too, Lewis."

"Ugh, you're right." Lucy rolls her eyes.

"Okay," I say. "We will finish our drinks and make a move."

"What about me?" Tom pouts. "I feel neglected."

"Come here," I say, launching myself onto Tom's lap. I feel a sudden bump, and he smiles at me and kisses me more. I am so horny and I know he is too, because I can feel it.

"Follow me to the bathroom in two minutes," he whispers.

I bite his ear. "I want you now."

"I want you."

I lift myself off Tom's knee and sit back down on the seat. Tom says, "I am just off for a ciggy," as he gives me a sly wink. I turn around to check if Lucy saw our little exchange, but she's too busy snogging Lewis's face off.

I rub my eyes to make sure I'm seeing this correctly. Someone Lucy has always been rude to, is now her conquest of the night. I glance at my watch, waiting uncomfortably until the two minutes is up.

"I am just going to kiss Tom goodnight," I say to Lucy as I stand up. She doesn't even pause in her making out, but she lifts a hand to wave goodbye to me.

Well, I'm glad Lucy is getting some action, even if it's not from someone I would have picked. I make my way to the bathroom, where Tom is waiting with his hand down his trousers. Several other couples are making out in the area.

Tom says, "Come on, follow me," and leads me to a fire exit door. We step outside into a secluded alleyway, with the light from the doorway scattering over the ground. Tom closes the door, plunging us into pitch darkness and takes my hand. "Keep following."

As I do, sounds of moaning and sighing surround us. "What's that noise?" I ask.

He just laughs and my face grows hot as I realise there must be a lot of people having sex out here in the blackness.

"I can't see a thing," I tell him.

"Shhhh, we are nearly there." He continues to lead me to the back of the alleyway.

"Where are we going?" I ask.

Suddenly, he stops and pushes me down on a hard, slightly curved surface. The bonnet of a car, maybe? "Go down on your knees," he says.

I obey, my heart thumping.

I hear the sound of him undoing the zipper on his trousers. "Pull my boxer shorts down," he says.

I feel my way to his waistband and slide my fingers inside, looking up towards his voice, although I can't see his face because of the dark. I can sense he is enjoying himself. Before I know it, we are kissing and touching one another all over our hot bodies. I undo my trousers and pull them down. Tom's hand creeps inside my boxer shorts and eases them down. Our tongues dance inside each other's mouths. Tom makes love to me on the bonnet of the car. He is so gentle with me and I feel like I am in paradise.

He finishes with a grunt. I sigh. Fuck, that was amazing. Tom gets his breath back and a cigarette flares in the dark, illuminating his face as he takes a drag.

"Did you use protection?" I ask Tom.

"No," he says. "But don't worry—I am clean as a whistle. Besides, we are a couple now, and I am only going to be making love to you, babe."

I sort of already suspected we were a couple, but hearing Tom say it out loud sends my heart racing all over again. I don't think I've been this happy in…well, maybe forever.

Tom's phone screen lights up as he checks it, sending blue light onto his face. "Fuck, Matt, it's 4 a.m."

Reality crashes back in as I imagine Jessica railing at me for being late again. "OMG, I better go, Tom."

We get dressed and make our way back to the club, only to find that the door is closed and secure. No music comes from inside.

"Well, I guess we'll just go around the side," Tom says.

A shadowy feminine figure approaches, tottering on high heels. I hope that it's Lucy, but Polly Easylay's voice comes out of the dark. "Oh, that's better. I just had my weekend shag and now I am ready for the long drive home."

"Why is the club door all locked up?" I ask.

"It's closed, darlings," Polly says. "You know it is 4 a.m., right?"

"Yeah, we know," we both say at the same time.

"Well, off you pop, then." Polly stumbles down the path in her huge shoes, trying to pull up her tights as she walks. "Goodnight, darlings!" she calls over her shoulder.

"I better go," I say.

"Okay, babe," he says, and we kiss each other.

"Hey, what are you to up to?" Dan's voice floats out of the dark. He and another man—Paul, presumably—walk up to us.

Tom says, "Just about to get a taxi for Matt. What about you?"

"We were just heading back inside the club," Dan says.

"I thought the club was closed," I say.

Paul says, "It is, but we are the owners and we can do what we like."

"Oh. Of course." I feel a bit stupid now. I'll just chalk it up to my tiredness, the drinks and the amazing sex I just had.

As Tom leads me around the building to the taxi rank, I catch sight of Lucy with her tongue down Lewis's throat, illuminated by the streetlamps.

I say to Tom, "Look at the new love birds. Shall we go say hi?"

"Nah. Leave them alone," Tom says.

Once we reach the line of taxis, I kiss Tom goodnight. "Love you," he mumbles against my mouth.

I try to feel his hot body, but he pushes me away and says, "I will call you tomorrow."

I say, "No, text me later."

As I sink into the back seat of the taxi, a wave of exhaustion hits me. My legs seem to float away from my body. A soft bed and sleep sounds like a great idea right now.

Finally, the taxi stops at my address and the driver opens my door to help me out. "That'll be ten pounds," he says.

"What?" I say. "Even though it's just a few yards from town?"

"Them's the rules, sir."

I grab a £10 note and hand it to the taxi driver. "There." I stomp off up the driveway. I just want to sleep forever.

I stumble up the stairs to the landing. My father peers out of his bedroom in his dressing gown. "Are you all right, Son?" he says in a low voice.

"Yeah, Dad." I slope into my bedroom, crash onto my bed and stare up at the ceiling. The room seems to spin around me. I close my eyes and sleep hits almost instantly.

*

My phone alarm beeping from inside my jacket pocket wakes me up. I grab it and look at the screen. It's 8:30 a.m.

"Oh, shit," I mumble. I am going to be late again. Even so, I just don't seem to have the energy to move. My limbs feel like they're made of lead.

But I know have to get my arse to work. I force myself out of bed, strip and run to the shower. After a quick shave, I dress in my work clothes and tiptoe down the stairs. There's no way I can drive a car in this state, so I run for the bus stop, my head pounding. I imagine Tom naked to take my mind off the pain.

The bus is packed and I find myself having to stand. I take my phone out to text Tom and make sure he got home safe. Then, I text Lucy to tell her I survived the night and I'm on my way.

The bus arrives outside the office block. I run up the steps and through reception, not saying good morning to anyone in the lift. I reach my floor and walk slowly to my desk. Each step I take makes me regret bothering to show up even more. Quitting my job and starting a toy shop sounds like an even better idea than ever right now.

Lucy appears next to me, grinning despite the bags under her eyes. "Morning, Matt. My head is spinning."

I set my things down on my desk. "Join the club, hun. Now, what happened to you last night with that Lewis?"

"You rang?" The post guy steps out from behind the door.

Lucy giggles, puts her arms around Lewis and kisses him. "I guess you could say a lot happened last night."

My eyebrows shoot up into my hairline. "So this romance survived the night, did it?"

"Yes, Matt," Lucy says.

"Well, I never. You and Lewis. You'll have to give me all the details!"

"So will you!" Lucy says. "Where did you and Tom go off to last night?"

I waggle my eyebrows. "He took me somewhere dark."

"Oh, he did, did he?" Lucy grins. "Well, you weren't the only one who got lucky this time."

"No way!" I clap my hands over my mouth in exaggerated astonishment.

Lucy giggles and tightens her grip on Lewis.

"Lewis, you'd better have used a party hat," I say.

Lewis looks confused. "Party hat? What?"

Lucy rolls her eyes. "Don't worry, Matt. He did."

"Well…" Lewis glances at his watch. "I'd better get on with my work."

"No, don't leave me!" Lucy whines. She grins and stands on her tiptoes and they proceed to snog each other's faces off.

I say, "Jeepers, Lucy! You suck the air out of him."

They finally break apart and Lewis says, "I will see you later, my little snow leopard."

"Okay, my little stud," Lucy says.

Lewis lights up like a Christmas tree. He blows her a kiss as he leaves and she does the same.

"OMG, Lucy!" I say. "Well, you and Lewis!"

"Oh, he's so good in bed, Matt. So dreamy!" Lucy fans herself. "So how's your Tom this morning?"

"I haven't heard from him yet."

Lucy frowns. "That's a bit funny, don't you think?"

"It's too early to panic. He's probably still recovering from last night. I don't blame him—I have the biggest hangover going! All I remember is the sex, Tom putting me in a taxi, and seeing you and the office clown eating one another's faces."

Lucy play-punches me. "He is not the office clown, Matt! When you get to know him, he is a lovely person deep down."

"Oh, I gather that you have already been deep down," I giggle. "Do me a favour; keep an eye out for the Wicked Witch. I just want to phone Tom and see how he is this morning."

Lucy opens the office door to spy through a small gap so she can see if Ice Queen Jessica is about. I phone Tom's number, but it goes straight to voicemail.

"That's strange. Maybe he's speaking to someone else," I say. "Oh, well."

"Ugh." Lucy presses a hand to her forehead. "I wish Lewis had stuck around to keep me company. I feel like crap."

"From the drinks, or from your spat with Polly Easylay? I don't think I have seen anyone challenge a drag queen before last night. Shame about the champers. But Polly's face when you threw the drink at her was priceless!" She sighs. "Don't remind me, Matt. There's only one word I have to describe her: vile. And what sort of a name is Bambi?"

I just giggle at her as she mutters "vile" under her breath a few more times.

"The cocktails were nice, though."

"Yeah, they were. But I am definitely feeling it this morning."

"Yeah, me too." I start to log onto my computer when my phone pings with a text from Tom.

Morning, babe! How about you meet me for lunch at the Coffee House? He ends the text with four kisses and a smiley emoji.

"Aw," I say to Lucy. "He wants to meet for lunch."

"Mm-hmm." Lucy nods slowly. I would have expected her to be a bit more enthusiastic, like she usually is, but I just chalk it up to her hangover. I text Tom back. *Great! See you at 1 p.m.*

Lucy and I finish our last file before lunchtime, and Lewis enters our office with a bunch of flowers for Lucy. She squeals and kisses him.

"Are you ready for lunch, Lucy?" I say.

"I brought my own today and I am going to eat it in the post room with Lewis."

I say under my breath, "That's not all you're going to be eating!" I say bye to Lucy and escape the prison of an office building.

Tom is serving a table when I arrive at the Coffee House. I stand at the counter and pretend to study the menu so I don't get Tom into trouble with his boss. I glance at him as he finishes setting the plates down in front of the customers and calls me towards him.

He whispers to me as he passes, "Meet me upstairs in the storeroom past the toilets."

I say, "Okay," and Tom goes back behind the counter.

I make my way up the stairs and find the storeroom he mentioned. I wait inside for a few minutes before the door bursts open and Tom enters, fully naked and with a beautiful erection.

I shed my clothes faster than I can blink, and before long, we are at it like rabbits all over the storeroom area.

"Oh Tom," I say, "I don't want you to stop."

"Me neither," he sighs. Sweat pours off his body like he's in the Sahara Desert.

My phone alarm goes off in my coat, signalling that I need to get back to work. Tom finishes and kisses me. "Thank you for lunch." He pulls his clothes back on and heads out the door.

I quickly get dressed and make my way to the bathroom to wash my hands. On my way out of the Coffee House, I catch sight of Tom, innocently serving a table. He winks as I walk past.

Tom's skill has done wonders for my hangover and I think that today might not be so bad after all. But when I arrive back at the office, Miss Bargain Boxed Shoes Ramscock stands at my desk, her face like thunder.

Chapter Four

I gulp as my stomach sinks down to my toes.

Jessica pierces me with her steely gaze. "Mr Storm, not only are you late returning from your break again, but you have managed to incorrectly format the sales reports you just handed in."

"Um…sorry?"

"I like them double-spaced and indented. I had to spend fifteen minutes fixing all your mistakes. In all the years I have worked for Gallagher & Masons, I have never seen poorer quality of work than yours!"

I don't know if it's the hangover, or if all these months of office misery are catching up to me, but my blood begins to boil. I clench my hands into fists. "I'm sorry my work isn't up to your *standards,* Jessica. And for the record, you never told me exactly how you wanted them formatted."

"If you'd been paying attention, you'd know! It's like you don't even want to be here."

My reckless anger rises and my mouth runs off on its own, saying everything I've wanted to say for so long. I laugh hysterically. "You're absolutely right! I hate this place with a flaming passion. I always have. And you know what? You can shove the heel of your bargain boxed shoes right up your ass!"

Jessica's face pinches with fury. "Mr Storm, you're fired!"

I reply, "No, I quit! I needed an excuse to leave this dump anyway."

Jessica says, "Well, your wish has come true! Now, get out right this second!"

I pick up a pile of files from my desk and shove them at Jessica. She fumbles and all the papers scatter on the floor.

I grab my coat. "Enjoy picking those up." I stomp out, slamming the door behind me.

On my way to the lift, I pass Lucy. Her eyes widen. "What's wrong, Matt? You look like you're about to punch a wall!"

I shove my hands in my pockets, just in case I do get the overwhelming urge to punch a wall. "The Wicked Witch of the Ramscock just fired me."

Lucy gasps. "Oh no, Matt! No!"

"I will text you later," I tell her. The faint sound of Jessica's heels clips along the corridor and Lucy scurries away.

The lift arrives and I quickly run into it before Jessica can show up. A hot tear falls down my face, followed by another. I press the ground floor and keep my hand on the button until it stops. I've either done a really stupid thing, or a really great thing, and I'm not sure which.

I take a deep breath to compose myself and walk calmly from the lift, past Vera the receptionist, who smiles at me. I make my way down the office steps for the last time. My sentence in that prison has truly been served.

I pause at the bottom of the steps, thoughts flying into my mind. I rock back on my heels for a moment, scarcely able to believe it. Did I make the right decision? Was quitting my job a mistake? Maybe I should go back in and apologise to Jessica, grovel at her feet to redeem myself to her. But she'd probably just laugh in my face, and I'd have made a fool of myself for nothing. Besides, even if she did let me come back, she'd make my life even more of a misery than she did before.

I wipe the tears from my eyes as I make my way around the corner. I take my phone out of my coat pocket to call Tom.

"Hi, Matt!"

"Hey, Tom." I sniffle.

"Matt, are you okay?"

I tell him what just happened and he's quiet for a second before saying, "Meet me on the bench in the park."

As I hang up, I receive a text from Lucy. *Are you okay? Do you want to talk about it?* She adds a kiss.

I text back, *I'm fine. Just upset about what that evil bitch said to me.* I know I wasn't exactly a model employee, but couldn't she have kindly offered to show me the way she wanted me to do things instead of yelling at me?

As I make my way to the park to meet Tom, I see a colourful poster on the side of a bus stop. It proclaims: "Start Your Future Now, and Make Your Dreams Tomorrow's Reality."

I pause for a second. Maybe I should take those words as a sign. Now that I'm out of the office, my life is full of possibilities. A ray of sun breaks through the clouds overhead as I resume my pace.

Tom is already waiting on the bench when I arrive. He stands up and pulls me into a hug. "It will be okay, babe."

I sigh into his jacket. "I know. It's just…all the years I have worked in that place and I still never got any respect from that woman. She hated me right from the start. Never even gave me a chance."

Tom comforts me as we both sit back down on the park bench. "Onwards and upwards, babe. Now you can find another job—a better one. One that brings you joy."

I say, "Well, I have always wanted to own my own toyshop."

"That's funny. So have I!"

A huge smile stretches across my face. Suddenly, being fired seems like the best thing that's ever happened to me. "Let's do it!"

"Yes, let's do it!" He touches my face and kisses me.

When we pull apart, he says, "Hey, there's something I need to tell you. You know a few days ago, when we went for a drink at O'Sheas and walked to the Melford Arms?"

"Yeah."

"Well, the Melford Arms was my parents' pub. My mother had an affair with the baker and left my dad and me."

I run my hands through Tom's hair and look into his eyes. "I had feeling it was. I'm sorry." I kiss him again.

"Yeah, well, it's in the past now," Tom says. "But the future is still to come. Come on, no time to waste. Let's go find ourselves a shop!"

"What, right now?"

"Yes!" Tom pulls my hand and lifts me off the bench. Excitement fills my chest. As we walk along the park path, I catch sight of the spot where we made love in the woodland. I nudge Tom, and the smile on his face shows that he remembers.

"Come on," he says and he drags me behind the bushes. Our mouths collide and the bulge in his trousers presses against my leg, waiting to explode. He places my hand on his trapped penis and guides it up and down, then pushes me on my knees and undoes his zipper. His penis emerges and he places it in my mouth, pushing back and forth—slowly to begin. As I suck, he groans and moves faster, and my body fizzes with the excitement of pleasing him so much. Before long, he pulls out and ejaculates on my face. He looks down at me and smiles. I find an old piece of tissue in my coat and I wipe my face clean.

He does his trousers back up and pulls me to my feet. We kiss again, long and slow, before

We head off into the town centre to look for empty shops. Tom says, "Have you got any money to put a deposit down for a lease?"

"I have a few months of savings I could use and I am sure my mother would help." Oh God, my mother doesn't know I've been fired yet. I'll have to tell my parents tonight.

Tom says, "Speaking of your parents, when do I get to meet them?"

"How about you come over next week?"

Tom grins. "I would love to."

"When can I meet your dad?"

"Soon, Matt. He is not in a good place at the moment. Mum leaving took a toll on him. Every day is a task for him to get out of bed."

"Oh, Tom." I hug him.

"Look!" he says suddenly.

"What?" I turn around to look in the direction he's pointing. A boarded-up building sits between a bank and a men's clothes shop. I walk up to peer into the windows. It's small, but kind of cute, and looks to be in good repair. A sign on the front says 'To Let'.

"Go on, Matt. Call the letting agent's number on the board," Tom urges.

The next few hours pass in a blur. The letting agent takes my details on the phone and comes to show us around the inside of the shop. I can almost see the shelves and racks of toys already. It's perfect. The letting agent lets me and Tom explore the shop on our own while she makes a call. We walk to the back of the shop and admire the place—the large windows, the slope of the roof. Tom glances at me. "What do you think?"

I say, "I think it's perfect. What about you?"

He replies, "Yeah, it's perfect. But I think we need to look around a bit more." He pulls me into a hidden corner behind an angle in the wall, and elation fills my body as Tom pushes me against the plasterboard and starts to kiss me. Our tongues lock together, and Tom moves my hand down to his waistband, pulling his neatly-ironed shirt out from his trousers. My hand finds his penis, which starts to get excited …but not for long, as we hear the footsteps coming toward us. I snatch my hand away from his crotch just as the letting agent says, "So, what do you both think?"

Tom sniggers. I say, "Could you give us a few more moments? We want to have one final look."

After one last circuit of the shop, this time without any kissing

Tom and I tell the letting agent we want the shop. She hands me a card with the landlord's contact details to pay the deposit. I'll have to talk to my parents about lending me the money right away. I can't lose this beautiful building when I've only just found it.

What started out to be a bad day has become a good one. When I arrive home, I head to the kitchen and tell my parents about losing my job.

My mum hugs me and kisses me on the cheek. "Things happen for a reason," she says. "You'll be on to bigger and better things soon!"

"Yeah, Mum." I grin. "And speaking of bigger and better things…I have some exciting news."

"Well, tell us!" my dad says.

After a long pause for suspense, I drop my bombshell. "Tom and I are opening our very own toy shop!"

My parents sit in silence for several tense moments. Then, my dad says, "Oh, Son, that's a big challenge to take on, don't you think?"

"No, Dad. A lot of people my age start their own businesses. All I need from you is some money for the deposit."

My dad purses his lips. "Leave your mother and me a moment, Son."

I head up to my bedroom. My parents' muffled voices float up from the kitchen, but I can't tell what they're saying. I cross my fingers. *Please, please, please say yes.*

"Matt?" my dad calls up the stairs. "You can come down now."

I descend the stairs, my stomach churning. My parents stand in the hallway, their expressions unreadable.

My dad glances at my mum, then looks back at me and nods. "We'll help you, Son."

"Thank you so much!" I hug them both, jumping up and down with pure delight.

"So when are we going to meet this Tom?" my mum says.

"Um…how about tonight? Is it okay if I invite him for dinner?"

"Yes, do that! We'd love to have him," Mum says.

I text Tom to tell him good news and invite him for dinner. A few hours later, the doorbell rings. I open the door and there he is, looking hot as usual. I get a sneaky kiss in, which turns into an impromptu make-out session.

I hear my mother call from the dining room, "Matt, what are you doing?"

We both giggle and I say, "Just hanging Tom's coat up on the hook!"

Tom meets my family and they take to him like a duck takes to water. He praises my mum's delicious cooking and she practically glows from his compliments. Time flies by and before I know it, it's time for Tom to go home. He says his goodbyes to my family and I announce that I'm going to give him a lift back to his place.

As we leave the house, Tom says, "I really like your family."

"I think they like you too. Am I taking you to your place at the Melford Arms?"

"Yeah, that would be great."

During the drive, Tom's phone pings. It's a text from Dan and Paul, inviting us to the grand opening of BillyJeans.

"Why not?" I say. "A night of clubbing sounds like a perfect way to celebrate our shop!"

"I tell you what," Tom says, "let's go and see the shop again."

I smile and put my hand on Tom's knee. He giggles. "Keep both hands on the wheel."

My hand wanders down to his groin and I can feel him getting turned on. "On second thoughts," he says, "one hand on the wheel might suffice."

We soon arrive at our shop-to-be, and we stand on the opposite side of the road to look at the signage.

"Have you thought of any names for our shop?" Tom asks.

"How about MT Toys?" I say.

Tom kisses me. "I love that name. Come here." He takes both of my hands, looks into my eyes and says, "I love you, Matt Storm. More than anyone in the world."

My heart leaps. "I love you too, Tom Sheppard."

We kiss again, not even caring who sees us at this point. I tingle all over. Tom suddenly says, "I want to share the rest of my life with you wake up every morning next to you."

"Tom, do you mean you want us to live together?"

"Yeah, that's what I want us to do."

We kiss a little more. "How are we going to afford it all?" I say. "The shop, and now a place to live?"

"We will get a small place, maybe a flat. I will pick up extra shifts at the Coffee House."

"You have it all worked out, don't you?"

"Not just a pretty face, am I?" He grins.

"Oh, I know." I kiss him.

Suddenly, Tom's phone pings. His face falls when he glances at it. "I have to go. It's my dad."

I ask him, "Shall I give you a lift?"

He insists on walking. As he is about to leave me, he says, "Ring the landlord in the morning and I will sort out a place for us to live." He lights up a ciggy and strolls off.

As I am walking back to my car, I phone Lucy to tell her my news. I talk for ages, telling her everything that happened after I left the office, from starting the toyshop to moving in with Tom.

Lucy remains quiet on the other end. I clear my throat. "Hello? You there, Lucy?"

"I'm here," she replies. "It's just…it's a bit much, you know?"

"I know it's a lot, but I know it's right. I can feel it."

"Matt, listen. I'm your friend, and I want to support you, but…don't you think this could be a bad idea?"

"What do you mean?" My excitement falters. I thought Lucy was going to be happy for me.

"Matt, you've known Tom for such a short time and now you're starting a business with him and moving in? That's…I'm sorry, but that's kind of stupid."

The words pierce my heart and I feel like crying. "Are you jealous of our relationship?"

Lucy replies, "I have no need to be jealous. All I'm saying is, I think you're making a big mistake. Tom might not be the person you think he is. You just don't know."

"Look, I thought you were my friend. I thought you'd be excited for me. Now you're insulting my boyfriend and telling me I'm stupid!"

"I'm not saying that. I'm just saying you're doing something that a stupid person would do."

"Look, this is my choice and you have no right to tell me it's the wrong one. If you're going to be like that, then I think…" I take a deep breath. "I think it's best if we end our friendship."

There's a beep. Lucy has hung up on me.

Oh, shit, what have I done? I call her back, but she does not answer. I drive home with tears welling up in my eyes. It's okay. I don't need people like her in my new life. I have Tom and that's enough.

The next day, I call the landlord. I can hardly keep myself from laughing with joy as I say, "We would like to rent the shop. How fast would we be able to have the keys?"

The landlord replies, "In a few days."

I hang up the phone with immense satisfaction. I am going to have a wonderful new life, and not even Lucy can stand in my way.

Chapter Five

A few days later, we hand over the shop deposit and rent. The landlord gives us the keys and congratulates us before he leaves. We survey the shop, which finally belongs to us. Aside from the shelves and the till we set up yesterday, the room is completely bare.

"There's one thing we haven't done." My voice echoes around the space.

Tom says, "What?"

I throw myself at him. It doesn't take long before we are half-naked and he is making love to me on the shop counter. He puts his hand over my mouth to muffle my sighs and groans so we aren't heard. I grab onto his arm muscles as he takes control.

All of a sudden, there is a knock on the shop door.

"Fuck," Tom says, jumping off me. "Who is that?"

"I don't know." The delivery we scheduled for our first lot of merchandise isn't due to show up for another two hours. We rush to get dressed. There's another knock and Tom tells me to go to the back of the shop to fix my clothes.

As I pull my trousers up, out of sight of the front door, I hear Tom say, "Hello, there. Can I help you?"

"I am Harry from the men's clothes shop next door," says an unfamiliar voice. "Just thought I'd come say hello to our new neighbours. Seeing as we'll be near each other whether we like it or not."

Tom introduces himself and he calls to me to come meet Harry. I button my trousers and come to the front door. "Hi, I'm Matt."

Harry looks me up and down. "Working up a sweat there in the back, I see."

I flush and Tom grins. "Yep, we're hard at work getting everything ready," he says.

"So, when will you be opening?" Harry asks.

"Tomorrow," Tom says.

Harry says, "Oh, you have got a fair bit to do to be ready tomorrow. I'll leave you to it." He walks away, muttering under his breath. I'm not quite sure what to make of that Harry.

The toy delivery comes right on time and Tom and I spend the next two hours putting everything on the shelves. I chuckle to myself as I place the ten boxes of train sets in the Boys section. Finally, the workmen come to hang our MT Toys sign above the door. It's blue and red lettering on a white background, and it looks smashing.

"All right," Tom says, looking with satisfaction at the sign. "Everything's ready. Now let's go celebrate at BillyJeans!"

I say, "Whatever you want. Your wish is my command!"

We switch off the shop lights, lock up and head back to our respective homes to get showered and shaved for BillyJeans' opening night.

*

We both arrive at the grand opening of BillyJeans, formerly known as Under the Rainbow. Dan and Paul are there to meet us at the club door, as is Polly Easylay, who seems to have made it her mission to ogle every man who enters the establishment.

Polly looks at us and licks her lips. "Aha, there you are. Now, where did I put my knife and fork?"

Tom and I start to giggle. I slip my arm around his waist. "Sorry, Polly, he's mine."

Polly sniffs. "So where's the vermin with the red lipstick got to? Has she been caught and put in her trap? She owes me *five hundred pounds* for my dress she ruined! When I see her again, she'll be smiling on the other side of her face. Tell her from me, sweetie—she's an old washed-out bag with no class!"

My heart aches as I remember my so-called best friend, Lucy. I wish she could have just been supportive of me. Polly looks like she's about to insult Lucy further, but then she sees someone she knows and walks off to have a ciggy with them.

Tom says, "Hey, Matt you okay?"

I take a deep breath to calm myself. "Yes, babe."

"I'm just going for a ciggy with Dan. You go on into the club. I will be right there."

Tom and Dan head off down the dark lane around the corner from the club for a ciggy, and Paul and I head inside. It strikes me as odd that Tom and Dan went down the alleyway when there was a smoking area right outside the club, but I decide I'm just being paranoid. They probably just wanted to avoid Polly Easylay.

I gaze around at the new changes Dan and Paul have made. They've switched out the hard wooden chairs for plush comfy ones and the lights are a softer golden colour. Paul tells me about how they want to buy a second venue in the not too distant future.

"Here we are," Paul says as we reach an area decorated in fluorescent pink. "Welcome to the Candy Lounge!"

My mouth drops open. "Wow, Paul! I think I need my sunglasses."

"Take a seat here. I will just go to the bar and get a bottle of champs." Paul smiles and heads off.

I lower myself into a comfy pink chair. I hope Tom and Dan are okay. They're taking an awfully long time to have their ciggy. An empty beer bottle sits on the next table and I absently reach over and pick it up. I start to peel the label on the bottle when Paul arrives back at the table with the bottle of champagne and four empty glasses.

"Oh, love, you're not sexually frustrated, are you?" he says.

"No." I smirk.

"Peeling labels is a sign, you know."

"Well, trust me, I'm perfectly fine with the amount of sex Tom and I are having," I say. "Speaking of, Tom and Dan have been gone a long time."

Paul shakes his head. "Dan's over there, talking to the DJ about his music set tonight."

Now I start to panic. Is Tom okay? What should I do? I'm sure he would have come straight back inside after his cigarette. Did he get lost somehow?

Just then, Dan shows up. "We're all set," he says to Paul. "The music tonight is going to be smashing."

"Have you seen Tom?" I ask him.

"No," Dan says. "Last I saw him, he finished his ciggy and said he had to take a slash."

"Okay." But even if Tom had to go to the loo, surely he'd be back by now?

Dan whispers something in Paul's ear and they both grin and giggle. I can't take it anymore. I need to see if Tom is okay. I make my way through the packed club and head to the toilet area. Male and female couples canoodle all around. I take my phone out of my pocket just in case I might have missed a message or call from Tom, but there's nothing from him.

Where the frig is he? I head into the men's toilets. The first door is unlocked, but when I push it open, I find a couple sitting on the toilet seat about to have sex.

"Oh, sorry." I quickly shut the door, my face heating up.

The other cubicles are all locked and there's no sign of Tom in the urinal area. "Tom?" I call, but there's no answer.

I head out of the toilets and make my way back across the dance floor to the Candy Lounge. Dan and Paul are sipping their champagne, and Dan waves for me to come and sit down. Before I do, I take my phone out of my pocket and open the screen to text Tom. *You okay? Where are you?* I add three kisses.

Just as I sit down next to Paul, Tom appears and says, "Hey, how's everyone doing?"

Dan and Paul raise a glass to him. Paul says, "We were just going to send a search party out for you, love. Well, I wasn't, but I think your husband was."

Normally I would be thrilled at hearing someone refer to me as Tom's husband, but my remnants of worry make it hard to enjoy myself. "Where did you go?" I ask Tom. Why am I being so paranoid?

Tom shrugs. "Well, I got to talking and lost track of time."

"I thought something bad might have happened to you."

Dan coughs and smirks at Paul.

"What?" I say.

"Nothing," Dan says, and kisses Paul. "So, how is your shop is coming along?"

"We are all set to open tomorrow," Tom says.

"This calls for a double celebration!" Dan says. "What is the name of your shop?"

"MT Toys," I say.

"Splendid! Let's drink to BillyJeans," Dan looks at Paul, "and MT Toys! Bottoms up!"

We all down our champagne. Dan burps. "Oh, sorry!"

Paul says, "Oh, I think it's show time."

The lights dim and Polly Easylay takes to the stage for her show. Tom takes advantage of the distraction to kiss me. Thanks to his caresses, I end up missing Polly's entire routine.

When Polly finishes her show, Dan and Paul rush up to the stage to congratulate her on her first show in BillyJeans.

Tom looks at his phone. "We better make a move soon. Big day tomorrow for us." He takes my hand and kisses it. "I am just going for a quick ciggy. Meet me outside. I will be quick, I promise you."

"Okay." I leave the club to wait for Tom outside.

The door security asks me to move to other side of the entrance, which is just around the corner to the pitch-black lane.

After a minute, two arms wrap around me and Tom's voice says, "Come on, babe." We move to the back of the club and kiss in the dark.

"Make love to me, Tom," I say.

"We have to go, babe. But I will make it up to you tomorrow."

I smile. "Yeah?"

"Yeah. We'll need to celebrate the big surprise I have for you tomorrow."

"A surprise? What is it, Tom?"

He chuckles. "Gotta wait till tomorrow, Matt."

"Give me a clue!"

"Nope. Otherwise, it won't be a surprise."

We say good night to each other with a passionate kiss and I think he's going to leave, but instead he pulls me back behind the club. My heart lurches—this is the place people call Shag Alley. With his hand touching mine, he places my hand on his raging hard-on, and in a flash, he pushes me to the floor and undoes the zipper on his trousers. He feeds me his penis and I do my best to please him. He groans and grunts, then ejaculates in my face, spreading warmth over my previously-cold skin. After that quick moment of passion, Tom heads off home and I stand panting on the pavement, wondering if all that was just a dream. It happened so quickly that I almost don't know whether it was real or not.

Tom heads off home. Tomorrow can't come fast enough.

*

On the morning of the grand opening of our toyshop, I float out of bed at the crack of dawn. There are still a few things we need to do before we cut the ribbon. I text Tom, *Meet you outside the shop in 30 minutes.* I tiptoe to the bathroom, shower, shave, and I am out the door. Morning is breaking and the sun is coming up to shine. I glance at my reflection in the rear view mirror. Matt Storm, business owner.

Before I leave, I look in the mirror to fix my tie; the image of myself all dressed up like a businessman makes elation rise in my chest all over again. I splash on a little aftershave and dart down the stairs, feeling a like a jack-in-the-box as I jump into the car and drive to my and Tom's new shop. A slight panic enters my mind as I draw closer—will Tom and I have enough money to survive on? As my father said a few days ago, owning a shop is a big challenge. But I know that, together, Tom and I will succeed.

*

I arrive at the shop and park outside. As I get out of the car, I see Tom walking from the other end of the street in his grey joggers, with his full package swaying. We have a morning kiss and I only just manage to stop myself putting my hand down the front of his trousers.

Tom hands me the keys to the shop, and I see there is an extra key on the bunch. "Hey, what's this for?" I ask.

He grins. "It's the key to the new flat I sorted yesterday for us. Surprise!"

"No way!" I throw my arms around him. Intertwined, we hug and kiss like never before.

"Come on," Tom says. "Let's open up the shutters. Fiona has given me a day off, but she still wants me to turn on the coffee machines for her, so I will have to leave soon."

We open up the shutters, add the last few pieces of stock to the shelves and shop is ready to open. We stand at the counter and admire all the hard work we have done.

"Let's get a picture of us together, outside the shop, before people start coming," Tom says. We head outside, just as my mum walks up the pavement. Carrying two large bags when she reaches the door of the shop, she says, "Take these love, they weigh a ton."

I take hold of the handles of the bags from my mum's cold soft hands. "Mum, what are you doing here this early?" I ask.

"I could not sleep with the all the excitement of you and Tom opening your shop today, love." She beams. "Good morning, Tom! I brought you both some bacon rolls."

"Aw, Mum, you're a star," I say. "I think we are almost ready to open. Tom and I are just going to take a picture of ourselves outside the shop. You're welcome to be in it if you like."

"Oh, that's all right, love. You're the owners. Is it all right if I go inside to have a look?"

"Of course, Mum."

She bustles inside. With the town starting to come to life with shoppers, Tom gives me a quick peck on the lips and holds his phone up, positioning it to take the picture.

"Make sure you get the sign in," I say.

He angles the camera up to capture the blue and red lettering. "Ready? Say cheese."

I say, "Sex!" as he takes the picture.

He breaks out into a giggle. "I am going to turn on the coffee machines. I will be back for the grand opening." He lights up a cigarette and walks off in the direction of the coffee shop.

I stand outside for a minute or two. Today has been so wonderful—a new shop and a new flat—and the morning isn't even over!

I head back inside the shop full of smiles. My mother looks up from where she is arranging the change in the till. "Oh, Matt, love! We are all so proud of you! I never thought my little boy would grow up to be so successful."

"Aw, Mum, I have never been so happy. I have the best boyfriend anyone could hope to have. And guess what? He got a flat for us to move into!"

Mum frowns a little. "Oh, Matt, are you sure? You have only known Tom for a short time. Having a business together is a big step as it is, but moving in together is a whole new level."

I say, "I know it's fast, but Tom is my world." I take my mother's hand. She has to understand. She'll always support me—not like that stuck-up Lucy.

She sighs. "Just be happy, love."

"Oh, I am, Mum. Believe me, I am." I hug my mother and kiss her on the cheek.

There is a knock on the door. It's Tom, back from the coffee shop. My mother goes to the kitchen part of the shop and I let Tom in.

"Everything okay?" he says.

"Yes, babe," I reply. "Everything is perfect, with capital P."

"Only twenty minutes to go."

"See, we have got time for a quick one."

He raises an eyebrow. "With your mother here?"

I giggle. "If only. Oh, I just told her about the flat."

"How did she take it?"

"Better than I thought she would." Better than Lucy did, anyway. "When can I see the flat?"

"As soon as we close the shop." I go to kiss him, when my mother comes running from the kitchen, holding the red ribbon. "Boys, it's time to open!"

We step outside to greet the gathering crowd of customers. My mum hands us the big pair of scissors and holds up the ribbon.

"You ready?" I say to Tom. We have another kiss. "Here we go!"

We both take hold of the scissors and lead the crowd in a countdown from ten to one. "…three…two…one…" The jaws of the scissors split the ribbon in two. "We are open!"

The first lot of customers stroll in through the door and Tom and I stand outside to savour the moment. Harry from the men's clothes shop says, "Well done, boys, the shop looks great. I can see you are going to be very successful here. If a horrible disaster doesn't happen, that is."

"Um…thank you?" I shake his hand and he grunts and heads back inside his own store.

"I am just going for a ciggy," Tom says.

"Okay, babe." I head inside to man the till, where customers are already queuing up to pay for the items they have selected. Children hop up and down with excitement as their parents hand them their new toys. An old lady smiles at me as I ring up a spaceman action figure. "My grandson will love this."

The shop is buzzing and the till is ringing with sales being run through it. Tom comes back from his ciggy and gets straight to serving people, helping them find things on the shelves.

"Matt, love, I am off," my mum says.

"Okay, Mum, thank you for your help!" I say.

Tom comes over and gives my mum a kiss on the cheek. She smiles at him, with a hint of sadness in her eyes. "Look after him, won't you?"

Tom replies, "Oh, don't worry, Elaine. I will!"

My mum gives me one last kiss before leaving the shop.

"With how well MT Toys is doing, you will soon be able to give your job up at the coffee shop!" I say.

Tom replies, "Soon. One day, babe."

The local press arrives to take a picture of our new shop— we are the first toy shop to open its doors in the town centre! Tom and I pose for the photographer and a reporter writes down my excited ramblings about how I've always wanted to own a toy shop, and how we came to open one.

*

Our first day of opening draws to a close. The last few customers leave and we cash the till up.

"We have had a very productive first day," I say to Tom as I tease him with my finger around his mouth. "Are we going to have a productive night?"

Tom giggles. "You've made me lose count now." As we count the takings of the till, he tells me to put them in the safe. He goes and has a ciggy and I take the cash and lock it in the safe.

I make my way to the back of the shop. After turning the lights off, Tom says, "Where have you parked the car?"

"Around the corner near the park."

"I will go and get it." He takes my car keys out of my hand. "What's yours is mine, and what's mine is yours."

"Oh Tom, that's so romantic. And how very true. I am so excited to see our new flat, and I'm excited for you to…"

"Pull the shutter down," he tells me.

"Oh flip, yeah, forgot about that."

Tom heads off to get the car. As I close the shutter on the shop and go out to stand on the pavement, I think to myself how lucky I am to have a gorgeous guy, and hopefully a great business and a flat. They say good things come in threes, and boy, haven't they just? A few moments later, Tom arrives to pick me up.

I get into the car. "Come on, then. Take me to our new home."

"Buckle up," he says.

A few streets away from the flat, Tom stops the car on the side of the road. "Babe, put this on." He hands me a piece of black fabric.

"What, a blindfold?" I say.

"Yeah. I want it to be a surprise for you."

I tie the blindfold around my head, covering my eyes, as he pulls off.

"Can you see anything?" he asks.

"No. But Tom?"

"Yeah?"

"Can I have a kiss?"

The car's movement falters and his soft lips touch mine.

As the car picks up speed again, I ask, "Babe, how far is it now?"

"We are nearly there."

Suddenly, the car stops and Tom announces we have arrived with a happy tone in his voice. My excitement is building up so fast that I think I will burst like a balloon. He opens the door and I hear him say, "Get out."

"Can I remove the blindfold now?"

There is a pause. "No, not yet. Put one foot out of the car."

I follow his direction.

"Now the other. Watch your head," he adds as I raise myself off the seat.

I step onto the pavement and the door slams shut. Tom's fingers wrap around my arm. "You're going to love this flat. I know you will."

"Can't wait. But please, can I remove the blindfold?"

He starts leading me forward. "No, not yet. Nearly there." He stops.

"What about now?"

"Yes. Take it off."

I slowly remove the blindfold and gaze at the front door to our very own flat.

"What do you think?" Tom says.

"Oh, Tom. It's lovely. Is this really our place?"

"Yes, babe. Who else's would it be?"

We both giggle. "I am lost for words," I say.

"Come on. Let me show you the inside." He reaches into my pocket and grabs the bunch of keys, which has both the shop keys and the keys to our new home on them.

Tom puts the key in the door and turns the lock. The door creaks as he opens it. "Don't worry about that noise. It just needs some oiling."

"I could use some oiling right now," I murmur.

"What was that?" Tom asks.

"I love the wallpaper," I say.

"I got another surprise for you. Close your eyes." I do, and he leads me for a few steps. "Now open them."

I do, and to my amazement, Tom shows me a room full of all the equipment we need to decorate our new flat.

"When can we move in?" I ask.

"Whenever you like, babe."

"Tonight."

Tom frowns apologetically. "I can't tonight. My dad needs help with his meds."

"Okay. How about tomorrow?"

"Yeah, sure. Let's move in tomorrow. But let me show you the rest of the flat."

He leads to me to the huge kitchen area, which is already fitted with furniture and appliances. "I can't believe how we have landed so well on our feet!" I say.

"Yeah. The guy who was here before told me he didn't want to take any of his stuff with him, since his new place had everything he wanted, and he would only end up throwing this stuff out. So I told him we would have it. I just thought you would like to decorate it first."

Tom shows me around a few more rooms. "What do you think?"

"I hope we are going to get to christen all the rooms, if you know what I mean." I pinch his bum and lead him upstairs into the bedroom. "Wow, we even have a bed!"

"Looks like we do."

"Well, we could start with christening our first room tonight."

Then we're kissing against the wall, and not long after, we're getting undressed and we fall on to the bed, our lips locked in a deep, passionate kiss. My hand moves up and down his body. When he pulls down my boxers, I do the same to him and we're fully naked on the bed and our bodies are on top of each other. He makes love to me, and it's amazing as always. He's such a master at his craft.

"Don't stop!" I say.

He climaxes, and we lie there naked on the bed, arms around each other. Anyone could have seen us, since the curtains weren't up on the windows yet. The room felt so hot with the memory of the lovemaking I just experienced with Tom.

We start talking about decorating the rooms. Eventually, Tom says, "Come on. I need a ciggy. Get dressed." He goes to get dressed in the bathroom—not in the bedroom where he just made hot passionate love to me—but I don't think anything of it and I get dressed too.

His voice calls from the living room. "Matt, are you ready?"

"Coming, babe!" I shout back.

"I will meet you outside." I hear the sound of the front door opening and closing.

I take one last look at our new home before we move in tomorrow. I wish it was today. I don't want to spend another minute apart from Tom.

I join Tom outside. "Oh, Tom, that sex was amazing. We've christened one of the rooms. Only four more to go." I giggle, but Tom doesn't. I grab him in an embrace. "Thank you for making all my dreams come true. I have never been this happy until the day I met you."

"Just think," he says. "Tomorrow, we will be moved in and never have to spend one night apart from each other."

We walk back to the car and I drop Tom home. He tells me not to let him out near his parents' pub, but just by the park entrance—he would walk home from here. We kiss good night in the car and I hold on to him. I don't want to let him go.

"I will see you in the morning," he says.

I kiss him again as he gets out of the car. He closes the door and I wind down the window as he reaches inside his jacket and lights up a ciggy. "Can I have one more?" I ask.

We share one final kiss before our move into our new home tomorrow. As I am about to pull off, I say to Tom, "I forgot to ask. Are you working tomorrow?"

"Yeah. Coffee House in the morning and then the shop in the afternoon."

I say good night and Tom heads off into the park. I drive home towards my last ever night of living with my family. I sit in my car in the driveway for a few moments, thinking about how just a few weeks ago I was single and in a job which I hated. Now, I have found the man of my dreams, we run a business together, and we're going to start living together tomorrow! Life is just great. I wish Lucy would have been happy for me and Tom, but I guess you can't have everything.

*

The day I have been waiting for is finally here, although I am feeling a mixture of sad and happy. More happy, because of the thought of me and Tom living together. Out of all the guys he could have been with, he chose me!

My dad knocks on my bedroom door and brings in some boxes. "There you go, Matt. To help with the move."

"Thank you, Dad. Where's Mum?"

Dad stutters, as though he's trying to think of what to say to me.

"Sit down, Dad." I indicate the bed.

As he follows my instruction, I think about Mum. I know in my heart she just could not be here the day I move out. She told me I will always be her little boy.

Dad finds the words. "Your mum has had to go and help Shirley's sister with something."

"Shirley's sister is more important than her own flesh and blood?" I say in a low voice.

"Don't be like that, Son. This is a big shock to us all, you moving out."

"Dad, I am thirty-five. What other thirty-five-year-old do you know who lives at home with their parents?"

"Look at your sister. She is nearly forty, and she's happy here."

I giggle. "Yes, Dad, but Loraine will be drawing her pension before she finds a man."

"Well, your mother and I want you to know this will always be your home. And if life doesn't work out with Tom, you know you're always welcome home."

"Thanks, Dad." It's the first time in a long while I have felt so close to my father. I usually get along better with my mum. But Dad is acting so caring, and I can see he is sad about the thought of me leaving the family home to move in with Tom. "Right, Dad, help me with these last bits of mine."

He places the final few items into the last couple of boxes I have left. With all my belongings packed into four boxes, my dad helps me to load them into my car. I close the boot and go back upstairs, while my dad heads back into the living room to catch up with horse racing.

"I won't be long, Dad!" I shout from the landing. "Just checking I haven't forgotten anything."

"Okay, Son," he replies.

I stand in my empty shell of a bedroom, with just my bed and my drawer unit left. It's as if I've been robbed of all the possessions from my family life.

I sit on my bed and gaze out the window, which looks down onto the garden. My mind fills with all the happy times we spent as family during summer days, sipping cold drinks on the lawn. I shake my head and laugh. Those were fun days. But now it's time to go.

I text Tom to tell him I have all my worldly possessions packed up and ask him to meet me at the shop. I get up off the bed. "Goodbye, bedroom. We have had good times in here." I close the door and make my way down the stairs to say goodbye to my dad. He is so engrossed with the horse racing that he shouts at the TV as if he was there in person.

"Bye, Dad," I say.

"Bye, Son," he says, not moving an inch so he does not miss anything with the horse racing.

I close my parents' front door and take one more glance at the house before I make my way to the car and drive off to meet Tom. By the time I arrive at the shop, Tom has already opened it up.

He kisses me when I walk in and I am all over him like a rash.

"Stop," he says. "A customer could come in."

"I just can't help it every time I see you," I say.

"Well, we will be seeing a lot more of one another now that we are living together."

I smile. "Oh, my clothes and bits are in the boot of the car."

"Cool."

"Before I go," Tom says, "Oh, I have something to show you."

I raise my eyebrows and Tom laughs. "No, not my penis. This." He holds up a newspaper.

I examine the article and it's the write-up we had from the Kelford Times on our opening day. We look elated in the picture, holding hands with smiles on our faces, and my mum and our first customers fill the background of the photograph. The accompanying text contains several quotes from me, though the reporter cut a lot of my gushing and rambling—probably for the best.

"I want to hang this on our living room wall!" I say.

"Okay, babe, I will drop them off at the flat on my way to the wholesaler's."

Fiona, Tom's boss, pops her head through the back door and asks Tom to go and get some plastic plates and knives and forks from the wholesalers—she wants to try marketing alfresco dining to the customers.

Tom and I have a little giggle, Fiona says goodbye, and Tom says, "I'd better be off." He kisses me goodbye.

Just as Tom reaches the doorway, Harry from next door pushes his way in.

"Hello, Harry," Tom says.

"Hello, Tom," Harry grunts.

Tom looks at me and rolls his eyes. He mouths to me: *do what Harry wants*. I nod and Tom smiles at me before leaving.

I say good morning to Harry, who is complaining to me about the council wanting to move the Christmas tree from its usual spot. I pretend to listen. My mind is more focused on my and Tom's first night in our new home.

The shop door opens and two more customers come in. Harry appears to be winding down his rant. "Let me know how you and Tom feel about this outrage," he says.

"Oh, we will," I say. "See you later!" As Harry leaves, I add under my breath, "I hope bloody not." All Harry ever seems to do is moan about everything.

I ring up my last sale of the day and clean the shop ready to open for the morning.

A few hours pass and Tom still doesn't arrive to pick me up. I ring his mobile, but my call goes to voicemail, so I hang up. I walk over to the window display and pick up a teddy which has fallen over. After rearranging a few things out of sheer boredom, I pick up my phone again and try Tom's number. Again, no answer. He must have gotten held up, but why hasn't he rung me to tell me this? Or at least sent a text. Tapping my fingers, I try Tom's number again, but there's still no answer. I shoot him a text saying: *Babe, where are you?*

A few minutes later, to my relief, my phone buzzes with a text from Tom. *I'm parked by the clock tower. Come over.*

So I lock the shop up and walk over to meet Tom.

"Oi, wait for me!"

I turn to see Harry running up the street towards me.

"Hi, Harry," I say wearily.

"So, how many sales did you make today?" He falls into step beside me.

I don't want Harry knowing my and Tom's business, so I quickly change the subject, even though it will bore me to death. "Bloody mess with this Christmas tree thing, isn't it?"

Harry goes off on his rant again, filling the rest of the walk to the car. When the clock tower comes into sight, I say, "Well, this is where my lift is." Tom sits in the car across the road. I hope Harry doesn't cross the road to talk to Tom—I just want to get home to our new flat. Luckily, Harry simply waves and says bye before walking off to his own car.

I open the car door and Tom is all smiles, mirroring my own expression. I lean over to kiss him, but as I do, I discover that the passenger seat is leaned all the way back. "Where have you been?" I say. "I have been waiting ages for you to pick me up. I've been ringing and ringing your phone, and there was no answer from you."

I sway back on my heels. "Tom, what has happened to the seat?"

Tom laughs it off. "Aw, it must have been when I was balancing the stock on there from the wholesaler's, and I must have forgotten to move it back up. You can just do that now."

"Oh, yes, that's what it must be." I lower myself into the passenger seat and pull it up to the correct position.

Tom says, "So, how was business?"

I tell him about Harry complaining about the council moving the Christmas tree. We both giggle.

"I am starving," Tom says.

I rub his leg. "So am I." My hand wanders down to his groin.

He jumps. "What the fuck are you doing?"

"What I always do," I say, taken aback.

"Don't feel me."

"Oh, sorry…I thought, since it was okay before…but I'm sorry."

Tom says nothing and lights up a ciggy.

"No smoking in the car," I say.

"This is my car, too. If I want to smoke in it, I will."

The change in Tom's demeanour shocks me. This is the first time I've seen this nastiness in his tone of voice. "Is there anything wrong, babe?" I ask.

"No. Should there be?"

"You don't seem yourself."

"I am fine. God, I'm starving. We'd better get some shopping in. The cupboards are like Old Mother Hubbard's—not even a bone in them. And we need fridge and freezer items."

"Let's stop off at the supermarket and do our first lot of shopping for our new home," I say.

As we walk around the supermarket, I get the impression Tom does not want to be here. It seems like it's me selecting all the food for the both us.

"Tom, is there anything you fancy?" I ask.

"No. Just get whatever you want." He walks over to the newspaper section, picks up a magazine and brings it back to put in the trolley.

"Shall I get some strawberries and cream?" I make a sexual gesture at him. He doesn't say anything, but at least he smiles.

We proceed to the checkout with all the things we need. Tom pushes the trolley out of the store to the car. As we are putting the shopping into the boot of the car, Tom says, "Where's my magazine?"

"It's in the bag with all the shopping."

He searches through all the different carrier bags, unsettling most of the shopping, until he finds his magazine. He hands me the car keys. "You can drive."

I giggle. "Oh, thanks!"

He jumps into the passenger seat and, like a kid with a new toy, he can't wait to open; he unwraps the plastic on the front of the magazine and starts reading all the celebrity gossip from front to back.

"I just need to take the shopping trolley back," I say.

"Okay, babe," he replies without raising his head.

Now that he seems to be in a better mood, I need to make our first night in our new home special and sexy. My strawberries-and-cream joke from earlier might just have to become a reality. I head on over to the fruit and veg counter and pick up a pack of strawberries, then go to the fridge and pick up a carton of cream. But cream will spill everywhere and make too much mess on our new bedclothes. I glance around the supermarket to see what else I could use. A lady passes by me with her shopping trolley and I notice she has a tube of squirty chocolate in her basket. That's it! Strawberries and chocolate—the perfect combination to eat off Tom's hot body later.

I pay for the strawberries and chocolate and I can see the sales assistant giggling to herself, as if she knows what I am going to use them for. She thanks me and says goodbye. I take a sly glance over my shoulder as I leave the store, and she's watching and giggling.

As I walk back to the car, all I can think of is Tom lying in bed with the strawberries placed on different parts of his body, topped up with a heaping of squirty chocolate. When I arrive at the car, Tom is still reading his magazine. He doesn't even ask me why I took so long. Maybe he didn't even know I was gone, if the magazine is that interesting.

I sit in the driver's seat. Tom lifts his head up. "What are you doing?"

"I am not sure of the way. I have only been to our flat twice."

"You know where to go." He snickers.

"I really don't know, babe."

"Ugh." He passes me the magazine. "Swap seats with me. Hold on to this. I don't want to lose my place."

"Okay." I walk around to the passenger side and he jumps over to the driver seat. He starts the engine and turns the stereo. We both sing along to the song playing as we travel towards our flat.

"I have a surprise for you after dinner." I say.

Tom keeps singing, with his eyes on the road. I guess I am wasting my breath.

We arrive home. He reaches over and grabs his magazine, then heads off to open the flat door, leaving me to struggle with the carrier bags.

"Oi, Tom, help me with the shopping!" I shout. "You can read your mag later! We need to get this food in the fridge and freezer before it defrosts."

Tom slowly walks back to the car. "It's your shopping."

"No, it's ours," I say.

He opens the boot of the car. "You bought far too much."

"Well, there are two of us."

We make our way up the stairs to the kitchen and place the shopping bags we managed to carry on the table. Tom hands me the car keys. "You can get the rest."

"Thanks. What are you going to do?"

Tom goes into the living room and continues to read his magazine.

I make my way back down the stairs to finish bringing in the rest of the shopping. There are another six bags left and I struggle to lift them out of the boot. One carrier bag gets caught on something sharp, which pierces the bag and the pack of strawberries. One by one, the bright red fruits fall out and roll into the gutter.

"For fuck's sake." Now my dessert surprise for Tom is ruined. I don't attempt to pick the strawberries up. At least the birds will have something fruity to eat.

I haul the rest of the shopping bags from the car and upstairs to the kitchen. Tom still sits on the sofa reading his amazing magazine, which he is unable to put down for just one moment to come help me.

"Babe, come and help me with the rest of the shopping," I say.

He just sits there. "In a minute."

I throw down the last remaining shopping bags on the table and place the final food items in the fridge. I hear Tom coming to the kitchen. "Aww, I knew you would come and help me after I put all the shopping away," I say.

He pushes his body up to me. "Look, I'm sorry for the way I spoke to you earlier."

I am holding a loaf of bread in my hand and all I can feel is his penis getting erect in his trousers, and mine reciprocating. We're pressed together like two slices of bread in a sandwich. I throw the loaf down on the kitchen work top. I am so turned on.

We start to kiss and both our tongues dance with one another. We can't resist it, and the next thing I know, we are ripping our clothes off in the heat of passion. We slide down the kitchen cabinets to the floor and Tom makes hot passionate love to me on the kitchen tile. We are both fully naked and he takes full control, making sure he pleasures me every way he knows how.

All of a sudden, Tom's phone pings and he jumps off me to get it. I remain lying there, hoping he is going to continue where he left off, but instead he shatters my hopes. "I have to pop out for a while. My dad has texted me. He needs some help."

I jump up off the floor, still naked. "Shall I come with you?"

Tom races to get dressed. "No!" he shouts at me in a nasty tone.

"Okay, there's no need to bite my head off. I was only asking if you needed any help with your dad." I pick my clothes up and take them to the landing, where I get dressed. I peep through the kitchen door and Tom is texting on his phone. I make my way into the living room, sit down on the sofa and turn on the TV. We were just making love and then he turned so nasty towards me.

Tom, fully dressed and with his phone in one hand, asks me for the car keys. I reach into my trousers and throw them at him. They hit his hand and fall to the floor.

Tom stares at me. His face seems to be carved out of stone.

"Sorry," I say. "I didn't mean to throw them that hard."

Tom's eyes narrow to slits.

"Tom?" My palms tingle. Something's wrong. "Tom, please say something."

Then, Tom jerks into action, moving at the speed of lightning. He leaps over the coffee table. And smacks me in the face with the full force of his arm.

Chapter Six

Pain explodes through my cheekbone, penetrating all the way to my heart. I choke out a gasp and place my hand on my face. Sparks dance in front of my eyes. Tears slowly well up. What just happened? Tom, my sweet Tom, would never…

I let out a couple of sobs before I dare say anything. "What was that for?"

Tom's jaw clenches. "You hurt my fucking hand."

"I just threw them at you. I didn't know a little tap would hurt you. I am sorry."

"Fucking fat pig." He grabs the keys and heads off to his dad's, slamming the flat door hard behind him.

I hug my knees and lie on the sofa, crying softly. My brain struggles to process. Tom would never hurt me. He loves me, I know he does. Did I do something to make him act this way? None of this makes any sense.

Finally, I stand up from the sofa and look in the mirror. The left side of my face is as red as a strawberry, with Tom's faint hand print indented on it. I go to the bathroom, turn the cold water on, and tear a few strips of toilet paper from the roll. I dampen the tissue and dab my face, hoping the pain will recede. It does, a little, but all the cold water in the world can't reach the ache inside my heart. After I finish cooling my face, I walk back into the living room

I have to distract myself. I text my mother to see how she is, and I tell her about my and Tom's new home. I don't say anything about how Tom just slapped me in the face. I start to unpack the boxes of my stuff and place the items around the flat, including a lamp, which I set up on a table near the window. My face still throbs with pain as I lie down on the sofa and drift off to sleep. My hand covers my sore face from the impact of Tom's blow, as if touching it will magically make it go away.

I am awoken by a hand brushing over my head. It's Tom. I flinch.

But instead of being angry, he caresses my shoulder gently. "I'm sorry," he says as he kisses my sore face.

I relax a little. Looks like the old Tom is back—the safe one, who cares about me. That incident earlier must have just been a fluke. I look at the clock. "Oh my God, it's four o'clock! Where have you been?"

Tom stands up abruptly. "You know where I have been. At my dad's. I texted you a few hours ago. Look at your phone."

"Where is my phone?" I must have lost it in all the fuss.

"Here it is. On the floor." He picks it up for me. I can see from the screen that there are two text messages from Tom. The first one says, *Just arrived at my dad's. He's not in a good way—hit the bottle again. Won't be long.* The message ends with four kisses. The second text is timestamped two hours later than the last one. *Won't be long. Just talking to my dad*, plus six kisses. I decide to take the kisses as an indication that everything is okay now.

"How is your dad now?" I ask.

"He's okay." Tom heads off to the bathroom.

"I'm off to bed," I say.

His voice drifts from the bathroom. "Okay. I'll be there soon."

I head for the bedroom and flip the light switch on. The bulb blinks and then goes dark. I sit down on the bed.

Tom comes in. "Why are you in the dark? And still dressed?"

"The bulb has gone." I quickly get undressed and jump into bed, pulling the duvet over me I turn onto my side.

He goes into the living room and comes back with the lamp. "Babe, plug this in."

I reach over to his side of the bed and plug the lamp in for him. He undresses, with his taut, muscled body in full view, looking like it was sculpted by a master's hand. I peep through the gap in the duvet, but soon he pulls the covers down and switches the light off. He wraps his arms around me, with his manhood pushing into my back.

I turn over and he starts to kiss me. I am getting turned on, although the memory of Tom hitting me still lingers in the back of my mind. But the pain is over now. Everything is okay. It has to be. After just a couple of seconds of making out, Tom says goodnight and turns on his side.

I am so turned on. I want more, so I start to put my whole body against Tom, but I get no reaction back. He must be playing hard-to-get. Like a solider going into battle, I run my hand down his side and down to his groin.

"Stop," he says, removing my hand. "I'm tired."

I jerk my hand back like I've touched a hot plate. "I'm sorry, Tom."

Tom scoots away from me a few inches. I feel a pang of hurt, but Tom's probably just having a bad day. Just a bad day. I roll over on my side and fall asleep.

I wake up on my and Tom's second day of living together with Tom still asleep. Half of his body lolls out of the duvet. I grab my phone from the bedroom cabinet and it's displaying 6:00 a.m. Wow—I'm up early. I'd better not wake Tom just yet; the alarm won't go off till 8 a.m. I place my phone back down and try to drop back off to sleep. I turn on my side, but it's no good. I shift to my back, but I just can't get comfortable. I carefully get out of bed, tiptoe into the living room and open the blinds. The sun's rays light up the whole space. What a lovely morning. We should have a busy day in the shop—the sunshine does bring out the customers.

I leave the living room, go to the kitchen and make myself a cup of coffee.

I consider cooking a full English, with some eggs and sausages, but I decide against it—the smell and the noise of the pan crackling would wake Tom up. I settle for sticking some bread in the toaster and I gaze out of the kitchen window while I wait for it to pop up. A magpie hops on the guttering of the building below and I gasp—seeing one magpie is a sign of sorrow. The toast jumps up, and I struggle to spread it with the rock-hard butter from the fridge. After I finish my toast and sweep up all the crumbs, I wander back into the living room; my eyes are drawn to Tom's jacket, which hangs on the hook. He wore it last night and it seems to be very dirty. I take a sip of my coffee.

"Yuck!" I forgot to put sugar in it. I head back into the kitchen and add the sugar to my drink. I stand and stare out of the kitchen window. How would Tom's jacket get so dirty? I sip some more of my coffee before throwing it down the sink. I really need to know what happened to that jacket. I leave the kitchen, head on to the landing and take Tom's jacket off the hook with careful, quiet movements—the landing is not far from the bedroom. I take the coat back into the sunny kitchen. Tom's jacket smells like him, but I also detect hints of an unfamiliar aftershave. There is also a green smudge on the front—a grass stain.

I put the jacket over my arm, tiptoe out of the kitchen and hang the coat back on the hook, making sure it's placed exactly the way I found it. As I make my way back into the kitchen, Tom shouts, "Babe, bring me my ciggies and lighter."

I freeze on the spot. I don't answer him at first

He shouts again. "Babe, bring me my ciggies and lighter!"

I reach into Tom's jacket pockets to find the requested items. "Okay, I have them!" At least it doesn't matter how his jacket is placed back up on the hook now—I have an excuse for having moved it. But I would like to get some answers from Tom. I bring the grass-stained jacket with me as I make my way into the bedroom.

Tom is sat up in bed with half the duvet off him and his full package on display. His muscled arms rest on the duvet as he fiddles with his phone. He looks up at me. "Why have you brought my jacket? I only wanted the ciggies and lighter."

I shrug, handing him the coat. "I thought you might have wanted it too."

Tom reaches into the pocket, grabs his ciggies and lighter and throws the jacket across the room into the washing basket. I take a deep breath. "How did you get that grass stain on your jacket?" I remember getting an identical stain on my own shirt when Tom made love to me in the park woods when we first started seeing each other.

"Get back into bed," Tom says.

I look over Tom's shoulder at the time on his phone and it's showing 8:00 a.m. "We have to be at the shop before nine."

Tom lights up his ciggy, folds my side of the duvet over and pulls me back into bed. I don't refuse; I am like putty in his hand. I lie next to him, thoughts going around in my head like a merry-go-round. Why didn't Tom answer me when I asked about the grass stain on his jacket?

As Tom smokes his ciggy, he tells me cuddle in to him, and I do, like a pussy cat curling up to sleep. Tom kisses my forehead as he takes a puff of his ciggy. I start to feel Tom's hot body. He pulls the duvet back over him and tells me to go down on him. I slither like a snake under the duvet to the bottom and kiss every part of Tom's muscled legs as I make my way up. I reach Tom's man tool and gently rub my hand over it. I can feel Tom is getting aroused, and so am I; I just want him to make love to me.

He moans with pleasure as I make my way back up his body. He finishes his ciggy and throws the duvet off us both, then rolls me over on my back with him on top and starts to take down his boxers as our tongues lock in a passionate kiss. He runs his hands down my bare thigh until he reaches the band of my boxers and puts his hand inside to slowly release them from my waist. He kisses my rock-hard nipples. I do the same to him and he flinches; he always finds it tickly.

He moves in and takes full control, as he always does when he is making love to me. I can see he is enjoying every moment as he pushes more. I just love every moment of it. He kisses me more, and then he climaxes.

Tom pants like a dog fisting for water. "Did you like your morning surprise?" He reaches over to light up another ciggy.

I pull myself up to sitting and cuddle in to Tom, trailing kisses down his shoulder. "Thank you very much," I say, as if he was offering a service to me, instead of being my boyfriend. I look at my phone, which, in the heat of passion, has fallen on the floor. The time displays as 8:45 a.m.

"Babe, we are going to be late for opening the shop!" I jump out of bed and rush to the bathroom to have a shower, still calling to Tom as I turn the taps on. "Come on, babe, get up. We are going to be late."

The water gushes over my body and I think back to the lovemaking Tom and I just did. I still want to make Tom tell me about the grass stain on his jacket, but it's probably best to leave it for another time. I dry myself off with the towel and walk back to the bedroom, where Tom has only just got out of bed, his naked body is on full display to me. He kisses me as he walks past. "I am just going into the shower."

I kiss him back and my towel slips off and falls to the ground. My hands move down his body, which is still hot from the energy he used. He places my hand on his bum cheeks.

"Tom, we can't have sex again!"

"Why not?" he says.

"We have to get to work."

He starts to kiss my neck and pushes me to the bed, and he is all over me, kissing my body.

My phone pings. I say, "Babe, we have to go!"

Tom's erected penis presses against mine. I push him off me, even though our tongues seem inseparable. "Quick, babe, get dressed."

Tom walks over to the underwear drawer and picks out a white pair of boxer shorts. His man tool is soon hidden away in the bright white underwear.

With us fully dressed, I say to Tom, "Babe, have you got the car keys?"

"Yes, babe. They are on the living room table."

I grab the keys off the table top and we have one final kiss before we start our journey to work.

We arrive at the shop and open up for the day, just as the clock turns 9:05. A few moments later, the door opens and it's Dan and Paul. They have come to see us in our new shop, just like we visited them when they re-launched their club.

"Wow," Dan says. "It's like being in Santa's toy shop."

Tom and I look at each other and have a little giggle. Paul says, "Oh, Matt, love, you could be Santa!"

Dan looks at me. "My apologies on Paul's behalf for comparing you to an old fat man."

Tom and I break down with laughter—not just at Dan and Paul's jokes, but at the happiness of being together with friends in our new shop.

Paul says, "You must both come and see our new drag queen. Oh, she is the biz. She puts the G into glamour, loves."

I say, "What happened to Polly?"

Dan nudges Paul, and they grin at each other.

Tom says, "Well? Tell us, then."

Paul says, "Well, let's just say that she was caught with her knickers and tights down on the wrong side of the law. So we had to let her go from BillyJeans."

"The new drag queen, Dolly Rimmer, is so much better than Polly," Dan says. "I think Polly had her day, like those old ships they send to the knacker's yard. Or something like that."

We all start to laugh. Paul says, "Why don't you two come along tonight? There will be a bottle of champs on ice for you both."

Tom replies, "Now that's an offer we can't refuse."

Dan and Paul kiss us both on the cheek. "See you tonight!" Dan says.

After they leave, I turn to Tom. "Babe, we can't go to BillyJeans. We have some decorating to do. I want to paint the rooms."

Tom flaps a hand. "We can do the decorating another day."

"Okay. I suppose another night won't hurt."

Tom heads outside for a ciggy and a burst of customers walk through our door. One of them asks me if we stock dinosaur action figures and I point her in the right direction. My hands move like lightning as I check out item after item.

Tom returns and goes to rearrange the window display. The shop falls quiet when the last customer of the morning leaves, so I take the opportunity to restock the shelves. As I line up a row of rubber ducks, I think of all the people who come to our shop to buy things not for themselves, but for their loved ones. Perhaps I should buy something for Tom to show him how much I love him. I want to make him happy, so he won't get angry again and…

No, he wouldn't do that again. Everything is okay now.

Still, I'm sure a present wouldn't go amiss. I place the last duck in position and call to Tom. "I am just going to pop out a minute, babe."

He grunts.

As I walk down the high street, I scan the shops to try and find one that might have a suitable present. I spot Harry a lurking few doors down from the butcher's and I cross the road, hoping he doesn't see me. I really don't want to hear him complaining about that Christmas tree again.

I pass a jeweller's shop and peer in the window. A gold chain and two silver rings glisten in the display. If they're not too expensive, that could be a great present—a necklace and a set of matching rings for me and the love of my life!

I walk into the shop and ask the sales assistant if I can have a look at the pieces. She kindly takes them out of the window and lets me have a closer look. The rings have tiny words engraved inside: *I love you forever.* My heart melts. These would be perfect! It's almost like they were meant especially for me and Tom.

I ask about the prices. The gold chain's cost makes me wince, but the rings are only made of silver and are quite affordable. The shop assistant places the rings into two gift boxes for me. I stow them in my coat pocket and make my way back to MT Toys.

When I walk in through the door, Tom is busy serving a customer. I'm desperate to give him the ring as soon as possible—I can't wait to see his face when I place it on his finger! But then an idea strikes me. Something this special should be presented in a special way. I will give him the ring tonight at BillyJeans, in front of everyone there. What a wonderful memory it will be when we're older!

I turn my face away from Tom to hide my grin as I walk to the back of the shop to hang my coat up. I slip my hand into the pocket and pull out one of the ring boxes. The beautiful silver sparkles inside. I trace the surface with my finger.

"Matt?" Tom calls from the till.

I quickly snap the box shut and shove it back in my coat pocket. "Coming!" I hustle to the front, where a middle-aged lady is enquiring about where the jigsaw puzzles are.

The rest of the day brings wave after wave of customers, most of them shopping for Christmas presents. Christmas seems to have snuck up on me this year. I suppose the excitement about all these amazing changes in my life has drowned out the excitement over the annual holiday.

When the day ends, Tom counts the money in the till and I go to the back of the shop to get both our coats. I press my coat's pockets tightly; the last thing I want is for the ring boxes to fall out and ruin the surprise.

Tom locks the door, while I wait on the pavement for him to finish locking up the shop. In my mind, I'm already at BillyJeans, presenting Tom with the ring, kissing him as the crowd applauds.

The town centre winds down for the night as we walk back to the car. Tom lights up a ciggy, the smoke spiralling in the chill wind. His jawline is sharp in the dim light, his lips plump as he blows white mist between them. I really am lucky to have such a fit boyfriend.

We arrive at the car and Tom stubs out his cigarette. "Babe, I am hungry."

"Me too." I waggle my eyebrows. "But not just for food."

"Well, we can do something about that appetite of yours after we have some pizza."

I start up the car. "To the pizza shop, then!"

Tom's phone pings, but he doesn't look to see who the text is from. When I pull up to the pizza shop, Tom says, "What topping do you fancy?"

"Any. Just so long as it has loads of meat on it." I nudge him.

Tom leans away from my touch. "Okay, got it."

Tom gets out and walks towards the shop door. He takes his phone out and appears to be checking it. As he enters the pizza shop, it suddenly occurs to me that he could just as easily have checked his messages while we were driving here. Why did he wait till he got out of the car before he read the text?

I rub a hand over my face. There's no point in being this paranoid. Everything is okay and I need to get that through my thick head. I reach inside my coat pocket and my fingers close over the ring boxes. I pull one out to admire the piece of jewellery inside. So simple and yet so perfect.

I see Tom coming back with the pizza and I quickly close the box and place it back in my pocket. I need to stop taking the rings out—it's too risky. I would hate to ruin the surprise. I reach over and open the door for Tom and he collapses in the passenger seat, lugging a ginormous pizza box. The smell of cheese, meat and sauce fills the car.

I can feel my eyes bugging out of my head. "What size pizza did you get, babe? That box is huge!"

"A large triple meat surprise," he says.

"Well, it's a surprise, all right. We'll have pizza for days!"

I have to set a blast of air going on the windscreen to stop the pizza from steaming up the car. As I head towards our flat, I say, "Who was your text from?"

Tom opens the pizza box and the wave of delicious smells hits me again. "Do you want a slice?"

Tempting, but it would be hard to drive with one hand. "No, babe, I will wait until we get home."

He shrugs. "Suit yourself." He stuffs a piece of pizza into his mouth.

I want to know why he seems so intent on avoiding my question. When he finishes chewing, I ask, "Seriously, who was texting you?"

"Oh, it was just Dan checking to see if we were still coming to the club tonight."

"Right, okay." If it was just Dan, then why did he try to hide it? Then again, maybe I'm making a big fuss over nothing.

With just few minutes away from home, Tom puts his hand on my leg. "Kiss me."

"I can't. I'm driving."

"Come on, live on the dangerous side for once."

Well, if he insists. "Hang on. I will find a safe place to pull over."

I park the car on the side of the road and Tom and I share a hot, passionate kiss. Without the air conditioning, the steam seeping through the pizza box mists up all the windows.

Our hands start to move all over each other's bodies, but it can't last. Tom gives me one last kiss and says, "Come on, hurry up and get us home."

I start the engine of the car. Tom devours another slice of pizza before we even arrive at the flat. As we hang up our coats in the hallway, Tom says, "I want to shag you, right now."

"What about the pizza?"

"Fuck the pizza." He places it on the stairs.

We strip right there in the hallway, our hands questing. Our tongues lock together. He strokes me with his soft hands. "Lie on the floor."

Like a solider taking an order from their higher officer, I do what he says. He lies on top of me and makes hot passionate love to me. It feels amazing; he knows his craft, and the size of his manhood leaves me breathless. We climax at the same time, the tide dragging us both under.

And then he's back to business, getting to his feet. "Get dressed, babe. Remember, we are going to BillyJeans so we can see the new drag queen."

And so I can give him a fantastic present, but he doesn't know that yet. "Okay, babe."

Tom throws on his clothes and goes outside for a ciggy. I remain lying on the floor for a few seconds, getting my breath back from that steamy lovemaking. When I finally drag myself up and get dressed, I can't help checking my coat pocket again for the rings. They're still there, of course. I'm so tempted to give the ring to Tom now, but it will be much more special at BillyJeans.

Tom opens the door and I quickly step away from my coat so he doesn't get suspicious. "Well," I say, "we may not have eaten the main course, but the dessert was divine."

"Indeed," Tom says.

We eat a few slices of pizza and store the rest in the fridge. Then, we share a kiss at the bottom of the stairs before I lead the way up to our bedroom. We both shower and get spruced up, and I phone a taxi.

As we get settled into the back seat of the taxi, I suddenly realise I put on the wrong coat when I left. The one I'm wearing is my blue jacket, while my black one is still inside on the hook, with the rings in the pocket.

"Fuck!" I say. "Um…babe, I think I forgot to turn the shower off."

Tom rolls his eyes. "Ugh. Go turn it off, then."

I open the taxi door. "Do you want me to bring your coat? It has gotten a bit cold out here."

"No, I will be okay. Just hurry up."

I dash inside and transfer the rings from my black coat pocket to my blue one. I smile to myself as I look at the spot where Tom and I just had hot sex in the hallway. I could get used to having dessert every night.

As I walk back to the taxi, I can see Tom talking on his phone in the back seat. When I open the door, he abruptly hangs up and tells the taxi driver to take us to BillyJeans.

During the drive, it's all I can do to keep my hands out of my pocket. My instincts tell me to keep a tight grip on the rings to prevent them from falling out, but I can't risk making Tom suspicious. It would ruin the surprise.

The taxi pulls up outside BillyJeans and Tom lights up a ciggy as we get out. He heads for the smoking area and I wait outside and look at the posters outside the club. One of them is for the new drag queen, Dolly Rimmer. I can't wait to see her perform. Dan and Paul said she was the biz. Then again, I suppose anyone would seem like the biz after Polly Easylay.

Tom returns to my side and says, "Come on, let's go in."

As we make our way to the bar, I say to Tom, "Please can we not sit in the Candy Lounge again. I felt like I was in Barbie's living room."

Tom laughs. Dan comes to meet us and gives us both a kiss on the cheek. "So glad you came! Let me buy you both a drink. I insist."

"Very kind of you, Dan!" I say.

"Anything for my mates. What would you like?"

"Pint of lager, please," I say.

"A vodka and coke for me," Tom says. Some irrational part of my brain is a bit annoyed that he didn't order a lager, too—lagers are our thing—but perhaps he just didn't feel like having one today.

Just then, a loud booming sound comes from behind the bar. Dan says, "What the fuck is Paul doing now?"

Paul appears by his side. "Hello, everyone!"

"What was all that noise?" Dan asks.

"I was just connecting one of the speaker leads into the bar area. Did you hear it?" Paul asks.

"Yes, I did. And so did the rest of the club. You nearly deafened us all!"

"Well, it bloody did not work." Paul smiles at me and Tom. "Darlin's, welcome back!" He snaps his fingers to get the barman's attention. "Cocktails all round, please!" He turns back to us. "What would you gentlemen like?"

"Sex on the beach, please, Paul," I say.

"Oh, sex on the beach, is it, love? I remember when I had sex on the beach. I got sand in places where the sun doesn't shine, I can tell you that much."

Tom and I laugh. Dan pulls a face. "I am sure Tom and Matt don't want to hear what we get up to on the beach."

When we finish laughing, Paul says, "Shall we go and sit down?"

I brace myself for Barbie's living room again, but luckily Paul has a table reserved just three rows back from the stage, perfect for viewing Dolly Rimmer's show. We all sit down.

Dan says to Tom, "Do you fancy a ciggy before Dolly comes on?"

117

Tom says, "Why not?"

The two of them head off to the smoking area, leaving me with Paul. The other man begins to talk about his and Dan's sex life, half-complaining about how Dan keeps asking him to try the wheelbarrow position. "I just don't have the core strength, you see. Honestly, it's like he thinks I'm a gymnast or something!"

I nod and smile, feeling inside my coat to caress the ring boxes. Now would be the perfect time to put my plan into action. Pushing away my nerves, I say, "Hey, Paul, would you mind helping me with something?"

Paul smiles. "Anything for you, love!"

I glance around, then pull the ring boxes out. I open the lids to display the rings. "I'm planning to give one of these to Tom tonight. As a sign of my love."

Paul presses a hand to his chest. "Oh, that's so lovely! You're going to make me cry!"

I slip the rings back in my pocket and take a deep breath. "I really want to show Tom how much I love him. So I want to ask you a massive favour. Before you announce Dolly's show, would it be okay for me to go up on the stage and give Tom his ring in front of everyone?"

"Oh, of course you can! Anything for true love."

A huge smile spreads across my face. "Thanks, Paul! You're a star."

Tom and Dan return, and Tom squints at me. "What are you two grinning about?"

"Oh, Paul just made a funny joke," I say quickly.

"Really? Let's hear it, then," Tom says.

Paul glances at his watch. "Oh my, is that the time? I need to go check on Dolly Rimmer." He leaps up from his seat and heads off backstage.

Nerves build up in my stomach as I sit in silence next to the man I'm about to publicly confess my love to. People begin to congregate around the stage.

Dan says, "You're going to love Dolly! She's a class act, I'm telling you."

"I bet she is," Tom says.

My hand shakes as I take a sip of my drink, willing Paul to hurry up. I want to get this over with before I vomit from nervousness.

The intro music starts and Paul walks on to the stage. My heart pumps as if it is going to jump out of my skin. I don't think I've ever been this apprehensive in my whole life. *Deep breaths, Matt.*

Paul taps the microphone. "Good evening to all you wonderful guests of BillyJeans! I hope you're enjoying yourselves here tonight."

A chorus of cheers echoes around the room, and Tom and Dan join in. I clench my hands into fists to try and stop the shaking.

Paul continues. "Before I welcome our very own queen of BillyJeans on to the stage, we have someone in the club tonight who has something special for someone special." Paul looks at me and beckons to me. "Come on up, Matt!"

I force myself to stand up and walk towards the stage. Cheers and whoops reverberate in my ears. Behind me, I can hear Tom's voice saying, "What's going on, Matt?"

By some miracle, I manage to walk up the steps without falling over. Paul hands me the mic and I clutch it with both hands, squeezing it for comfort. Dozens of pairs of eyes gaze at me.

I clear my throat. "H-hello, everyone."

"Hello!" a few people say back. One man in the front row gives me a nod and a thumbs-up.

I suck in a breath. It's okay—these people are on my side. I try to draw strength from their encouragement. Time to speak right from the heart. "A short time ago, I fell in love with the hottest, fittest guy in Kelford. Yes, Tom Sheppard, that's you, and I want everyone to know just how much I am in love with you."

Tom stares at me, his face an unreadable mask. My stomach sinks, but there's no going back now. I put my hand inside my pocket and bring out the two gift boxes containing my and Tom's 'I love you forever' rings. "Tom, could you come and join me up here, please? I have something I want to give you."

Tom just sits there like a statue. Dan reaches across and pushes him, and he finally stands up and makes his way to the stage, his movements jerky and robotic. The club cheers as he mounts the steps.

He makes his way over to me, smiling awkwardly, but his tight jaw betrays his displeasure. In a soft voice that no one but me can hear, he whispers, "What the fuck are you doing?"

My breath hitches. I thought Tom would be happy, that he'd appreciate my confession, but he seems to be angry. But I have to go through with this if I don't want to embarrass myself in front of everyone. I open one of the gift boxes and the silver ring catches the light. "I got this for you to show how much you mean to me, babe," I say into the microphone. I pluck the ring from its case and slip it onto his finger.

As the audience goes nuts, Tom replies in the same quiet voice, "I don't need a ring to show how much I love you. You fucking idiot. You have shown us right up now."

His words are like swords stabbing into my heart. I swallow. I don't want to cry in front of everyone. Mercifully, Paul takes the microphone back from me. "Oh, loves, I am going to cry and all my makeup is going to run! Poor Dolly Rimmer—she's going to have to try and top that!"

I scurry back to our table as fast as I can, with Tom at my heels. I slump in my seat, swallowing down the lump in my throat. I won't cry.

Tom pounds back his drink in one go. He looks at me with a dark expression and shakes his head. Dan looks a little confused, but he has the good sense to say nothing.

Paul dashes off the stage to see what's wrong. He whispers in Dan's ear, his face concerned. Dan lightly pushes Paul back into his seat, ready to watch Dolly's show.

"I need a ciggy," Tom says.

"And I need the toilet," I say. That's not true, but I need a place to break down without anyone seeing.

Unfortunately, the smoking area at the back is right next to the toilets, so Tom and I end up walking together. His jaw is locked tight and a vein stands out on his neck.

I must have really upset him. As we pass into the deserted corridor that leads to our destinations, I say, "Babe, what's wrong?"

Without warning, Tom grabs hold of me and pushes me against the brick wall of the club, pressing one hand into my throat.

Chapter Seven

Blood roars in my ears and my hands scrabble to make Tom loosen his grip. "You're…hurting me!" I choke out.

"What the fucking hell did you humiliate me for in front of everyone, then?" His spittle hits my face.

No, this can't be happening, not again. It was just a fluke the first time. It can't be happening again. "I didn't…humiliate you. I wanted to prove…how much I love you…now please…let me go!"

Tom pushes more and I gag. His twisted face blurs as my eyes fill with tears. "*Stop!*" I scream.

Tom lets go and he heads out to the smoking area. I sag back against the wall, massaging my aching throat, sucking in huge gulps of air.

I pause and take my phone out of my pocket to call my mum and tell her what's happened, but my fingers freeze two inches from the screen. In the end, I shove the device deep back into my pocket. I know she will only worry, tell me to leave Tom or something horrible like that. Tears pour down my face. But…Tom loves me! I know he does.

So why did he do that? I must be going insane.

When my legs start working again, I run into the toilet, unable to contain my sobs any longer. A couple of guys stare at me as I flee into a cubicle. I lock the door and sit on the toilet seat, hugging my legs, rocking back and forth as I cry. How did my plan to show Tom I love him end up going this wrong? At least the two guys I saw on my way in left pretty quickly. Everyone wants to see Dolly's show, so they leave me to break in peace.

A few minutes later, the main toilet door opens and I hear someone walking across the floor. Someone unzips their fly and liquid tinkles into a urinal.

"I know you're there, you fucking fat bastard."

A buzz goes down my spine and I raise a hand protectively to my throat.

"Oi, fatty," Tom continues. "I know you're there."

I remain quiet. His footsteps walk over to my cubicle and a pair of black shoes stop outside my door. He bangs on the door, making it rattle. "Why the fuck aren't you answering me?"

I whimper, fresh tears welling up. "Tom, please don't."

The door flies open with a crash and Tom's standing there, glowering at me. I let out a cry. I must have not locked the door properly! He raises his hand as if he's going to hit me, and I curl into a ball, my back pressing into the toilet cistern. "Please, Tom, don't hit me!"

Tom grabs hold of my shirt and begins to try and pull me off the toilet seat. I put my feet on the floor to keep from falling to the tile. "Stop! You're going to rip my shirt!"

Tom grips my arm and manhandles me to my feet. He takes the ring off and shoves it in my face. "What the fuck do I want a ring for I am not going to marry you? Do you really think I want to spend the rest of my life with an overgrown fucking beach whale?"

My whole body shakes. Tom's going to hit me again. I need to get out of here, but I can't with him holding on to me and blocking the doorway.

Tom says, "Here's what I think of the ring you gave me." He flings it behind him and I hear a *ting* as it rolls across the floor. His spit flies in my face as he screams, "Now fuck off away from me!"

I whimper some more and finally gain enough control to say, "Why are you being like this? I only wanted to show you how much I love you. Why, why, Tom?"

"You fucking showed me up, is why."

"I love you, Tom! I wanted everyone to know, that's all!"

Tom raises his hand and I cower away from him. He's going to hit me! But instead, he just says, "Well I don't love you. Now, fuck off." A glob of his warm saliva hits me in the face. He undoes his fly and wiggles his penis at me before doing his zip up again. "Don't expect to ever see it again!"

With one final shove which knocks me into the toilet cubicle wall, Tom storms out of the toilets. I sit there trembling until I can make my limbs work. I have to get out of here. I have to get safe.

I stumble out of the toilets, bumping into several men on the way out. I barely register them. A mixture of Tom's warm saliva and my own tears runs down my face I wipe my face as I enter back into the club area, heading for the exit as fast as I can. The air seems to suffocate me. Dolly Rimmer is on stage and she must have spotted me leaving because her voice booms over the speakers: "Oh, looks like that guy has a date on Dick Finder."

Laughter echoes around me. The club door bangs against the wall as I push it open. I run and run until I can't any longer. I collapse on a bench just opposite the clock tower and sit there bawling my eyes out.

A pair of workmen glance at me as they string Christmas lights across a shop front. Many of the other shops already have their decorations up. The cheery twinkling bulbs seem so random and out-of-place in this nightmare that I almost laugh through my tears. The man I love just turned into a monster, but life goes on for the rest of the world.

In the depths of my mind's confusion, I have a vague notion that I should call a taxi. I take my phone out of my pocket, but then I put it back. I don't want the taxi driver to wonder why I'm so upset—or worse, ask me about it. I raise myself from the bench and automatically head in the direction of the flat.

As I am walking, I get the urge to remove my ring and throw it in a nearby rubbish bin, but the sparkling silver doesn't deserve that. I take its box out of my pocket and nestle it inside with shaking hands. I pass the coffee shop where Tom and I first set eyes on one and another, and memories crash into my brain. If only I could rewind my life to before things got this complicated, back when it was just me and a hot man looking at each other across a counter, dreaming of what could be.

I reach the front door of the flat and hurry inside. I race up the stairs like a rat up a drainpipe. Once in the bedroom, I peel my sweat-soaked shirt off. My face is puffy and red in the mirror. I brush my fingers over the purple bruise forming on my neck. Oh, shit.

I crawl under the covers and lie there, shivering, tears and snot running down my face. God, I feel disgusting. This can't be happening. I'll just wake up tomorrow and everything will be back the way it should be. Tom will love me. The bruise will be gone. Everything will be okay.

Despite my exhaustion, I lie awake for hours. Dread creeps up on me as I realise that Tom will be back soon. I don't want him to hurt me again. I should've gone to my parents' house instead, but I just couldn't think straight. Now I curse my own stupidity.

I hear a car engine outside the window. I get out of bed and hurry over to the window. Tom is getting out of a taxi on the road below, his face illuminated by the streetlamps. He looks up at the bedroom window. A stab of fear goes through me and I run and jump back into bed, pulling the duvet over me. The soft blanket provides a small sliver of comfort. I feel like a little child, hiding under the covers to escape the monster under the bed. Except now I know that a duvet isn't an impenetrable shield.

I hear the front door open. I glance at my phone's clock. It's 4:00 a.m.—over three hours since I left BillyJeans. It feels much longer than that.

The stairs creak and Tom's shoes thump on each step. I curl into a ball, but he doesn't come into the bedroom straight away. I hear him moving around, from the kitchen to the living room to the bathroom. His footsteps fall silent.

After about twenty minutes, I creep out bed and peep through the crack in the door. No sign of him. He's taking an awfully long time in the bathroom.

At last, the bathroom door opens with a thud. I dash back into bed. I can hear Tom muttering to himself, and a few scuffling noises like he's dumping his shoes and jacket on the floor. I can't make out his words, but their slur indicates that he's quite drunk.

The bedroom door opens. I close my eyes tight, my body stiffening. Maybe if I pretend to be asleep, he'll leave me alone.

The mattress sags as he sits down. "Oi, you awake?"

I fight to make my breathing steady. *I'm asleep, I'm asleep, I'm asleep.*

He taps the duvet cover. "Oi, fat bastard, are you awake?"

I remain quiet, silently begging him to go away.

The duvet cover whips off my body, dousing me in cold air. A hand closes around my shoulder and wrenches me onto the floor. I cry out as my body crashes into the carpet. "What the fuck are you doing, Tom?"

He replies, "Get the fuck out of my bed. I don't want you in here. And by the way, I am not working in that stupid toyshop anymore. You're on your own."

I gasp as I pull myself back up off the floor, standing on shaky legs. Despite my fear, a burst of anger builds up inside me. "Why are you still being so nasty to me? I said I was sorry about tonight. You're overreacting about something so tiny! It was only a ring, for crying out loud. And even if I did upset you, you're way too drunk to have a proper conversation about this now. We can talk about it in the morning."

Tom shoots to his feet. "No! I want to fucking talk about it *now*."

I don't reply to Tom and climb back into bed. He's not going to push me out of this flat that I'm helping pay for. I then find the courage inside me to say, "Well, I don't want to talk about it now. Goodnight, Tom."

Tom gets into his side of the bed and his hands push into my back as he tries to shove me out again. I roll over so that I'm face-to-face with him. "Will you stop? I am trying to go to sleep."

His palm crashes into my face and an explosion of pain rips through my jaw. I scream, fire racing across my cheek. His knee collides with my shin and he pushes me over the edge of the mattress and onto the floor. My body aches and tears well up in my eyes. I just want this nightmare to end; I want my Tom back.

"That's it," I say, trying to inject some venom into my voice with the dying embers of my earlier rage. "I have had enough, Tom. There was no need to hit me again."

Tom does not say anything; he just lies there, still as a statue. I grab my pillow and head out to the living room, where I make a bed for myself on the sofa. A glance in the mirror shows a red handprint on my cheek, overlapping with my existing bruise. What have Tom and I become?

I lay my head down on my pillow and the tears start to fall again as I cry myself to sleep.

*

The next day, I am woken by Tom's soft voice. "Matt, I am sorry, babe."

I look up at him and hold my pillow in front of my chest like a shield. Soft morning light frames his silhouette, but I haven't forgotten his devilish actions last night. "Tom, this can't go on. I am not a human punching bag."

"No, I know that, babe. I was just shocked that you gave me a ring, that's all."

"I don't think any amount of shock merits hitting me and spitting in my face. No, Tom, I have had enough. I don't think you love me half as much as I love you. If you did, you wouldn't have acted like you did last night, let alone thrown away the gift I got for you."

Tom laughs nervously. "I am truly sorry, babe. I picked the ring up after you left."

I glance at Tom's finger. "Oh really? Then where is it?"

"In my coat pocket. Where's yours? You're not wearing one either."

"In the box in my jacket pocket."

Tom dashes to the pocket of my jacket to fetch my ring and places it back on my finger

Tom smiles. "Come back to bed then, and when we get up, I will put my ring back on. Okay, babe?"

"Well…" I do love him, and he seems to be sorry. Do I dare hope that Good Tom is back? "Okay."

He gently takes my hand and places it down his boxer shorts to feel his penis which is starting to get erected. I quickly jerk my hand back. I'm not sure I'm ready for that yet when he's only just started being nice to me again.

He bends down and kisses my head and face. My bruise is still tender from last night, but I can almost ignore the lingering soreness as a tingle runs across my skin at Tom's touch. He presses his mouth to mine and our tongues start to dance. He pulls away. "Come on. Come back to bed, so I can show you how sorry I am."

"Okay. I will be there in a minute."

Tom heads back to the bedroom. "Don't be long!" he calls.

I stare out of the living room window at the bright blue sky outside, my mind racing. If I'd been more sensible yesterday, I could have gone and moved back in with my family. My dad did say I could come back any time. But now Tom seems to be good again. Maybe his bad behaviour was just growing pains and now everything will be okay.

"Matt, come on!" Tom calls.

I reply, "Coming now."

As I stand up to go back to the bedroom, I hear a ping from a phone. Mine is lying on the living room table, but there aren't any notifications on it. So it must be Tom's phone. Another ping sounds and I'm pretty sure it came from Tom's jacket, which is still crumpled on the floor from last night.

I don't know quite when I got so paranoid, but I cross to Tom's coat and get his phone out of his pocket. There are two text messages displayed on the screen—one from a guy called Finn and another from someone called Jack. My body judders. I want to know what the messages say, but the preview doesn't show the actual text—just the names. And Tom's phone is locked. Could Tom be…?

No, he wouldn't cheat on me. He's a good person.

Just out of curiosity, I check all of the coat pockets for the ring. It's not there. A buzz goes down my spine. Tom lied to me.

My heart pounds as fast as a terrified jackrabbit, but I don't reply. I turn the key as silently as I can and the door slightly creaks as I open it. The morning sun pours into the dark hallway and the light blinds me for a moment as I step outside. I feel in my coat pocket for my car keys and fish them out. The cold wind doesn't help the pain from Tom's ferocious attack on me last night— it just makes it worse.

I climb into my car and place the key into the ignition. Twisting my wrist makes the pain flare up again and I yelp. My hand hovers near the radio—some morning tunes may take my mind off the aches, even just for few minutes—but I decide against it. Silence would be more fitting right now. I slide down into the seat and my mind wanders back to last night at BillyJeans. How could Tom, my lovely Tom, be the perfect lover one minute and then turn into an evil monster the next?

I pull the mirror down from its holder and gaze into it. The redness on my face doesn't seem as bad as I thought. I touch my injuries and let out a yelp—my face is still tender and swollen. The last few hours have engraved Tom's temper all over my body. I feel an ache on my left shoulder. Pulling my T-shirt down and glancing into the mirror, I see a cascade of bruises spilling over my shoulders—too tender to touch even to rub cream on them. I fix my T-shirt so my injuries are not exposed and fold the mirror back into its holder.

It's going to be Christmas season in a few days. How am I going to explain these bruises to my family? My mind floods with excuses—stock fell on me, a door hit me in the face, I tripped on the pavement. But people would be able to tell I'm lying. I've never been good at lying.

As the clouds start to gather and the sun's rays dim, I open the car door and place one foot on the concrete kerb. The paper boy slows his bike down as be approaches me, copies of the Gossip of Kelford lying limp in his bag. "Hey, mate, are you all right?"

I shake my head. "I'm fine."

The boy looks sceptical, but he shrugs and rides on. I heave myself out of the seat and close the car door, my body kicking with pain all over as if I just went six rounds with Mike Tyson.

The door stands ajar when I arrive back at the flat. I step inside and close it quietly, then tiptoe back up the stairs, pressing a hand to my aching chest as though that will stop my heart from breaking.

Tom calls my name as I reach the landing. I reach into his jacket and fish his phone out.

Tom shouts from the bedroom, "Babe, what are you doing? Get in here!"

I take a deep breath and head into the bedroom with Tom's phone. "Here, babe. You have some text messages. From two guys."

"Oh." Tom snatches his phone from me and places it on the bedside table face down. "Thanks. But never mind that. Come back to bed." He grins and flashes his erected penis at me.

"Um…I'm not sure that's a good idea. It's a bit late. The day will be gone soon." Truth be told, I'm still a bit wary of him. Especially since he seems to want to hide his phone from me.

Tom laughs. "You won't be wasting your time, trust me."

"Aren't you going to see who your text messages are from?"

"Later, later. Get back into bed."

"No, Tom. I need to sort out the Christmas decorations. When I was walking through the town last night, I saw some people putting up lights. Made me realise Christmas is closer than I thought. We need to get into the festive spirit."

Tom laughs again. "So you're not in the mood for sex."

"No, not yet."

Tom's smile drops off his face. "Well, okay then." He grabs his phone and flops back on the bed. "Go make me some coffee, babe."

I go to follow his order, fuming a bit that he didn't even say please. But at least he's not hitting me anymore. As I create the brew just the way Tom likes it, I can't help thinking about Finn and Jack. They could just be friends of Tom's, but would he hide his phone from me if it was really nothing to worry about?

When I walk back into the bedroom, Tom is still on his phone, but he is quick to place it face down on the bed. I hand Tom his coffee and snatch his phone up in one swift movement. To my elation, it didn't have time to lock itself. Tom's home screen spreads out before me, the messages app right within my grasp.

"What fuck are you doing?" Tom's coffee sloshes onto the duvet as he dives for the phone.

I back up, holding the device out of his reach. "Who are Finn and Jack?"

Tom blinks at me and his mouth opens and closes a couple of times before he says, "They're just some guys who used to work at the Coffee House. I haven't seen them in months."

"So you're not sleeping with them behind my back, then?"

"N-no, of course not. Now please give me my phone back."

I slam my finger onto the messages app Finn and Jack are the two most recently messaged contacts. The latest message from Jack, sent just a few minutes ago, reads, *Yeah, last night was amazing as always! By the way, you forgot your ring I found it on my bedroom floor.* The most recent from Finn says, *So we're still on for meeting today at mine?* With a winky face and an eggplant emoji.

I feel like a whole set of knives has been stabbed into my heart. I look up at Tom just as he grabs the phone from me and drives his fist into the side of my head. My ears ring and I stumble to the floor, my head spinning.

"They're lying," Tom rasps from above me. "They're just jealous."

Tears squeeze out of my eyes. "Those didn't seem to be jealous messages, Tom. I don't even know them, but you sure do."

"You're so fucking paranoid!" Tom's voice suddenly escalates to a yell. "Why can't you just believe me? Why do you have to question everything I do?"

"Because you're a liar!" I shout back, my head throbbing. "And you know what? I…I am going back home to live with my parents!"

"Fuck off, then!" His spit sprays over my face.

"I will!" I walk out of the bedroom and slam the door behind me wiping Tom's hot spittle from my face.

I text my mum to tell her I am on my way over, my fingers pushing the keys so hard that I'm surprised I don't break my phone. My ear and head pulse with pain, so I wet a facecloth in the bathroom and hold it over the injury to ease the soreness. I do a mental run-through of the bare minimum I need to bring with me to my parents' house—change of clothes, wallet, laptop. I don't want to stay here any longer than necessary.

The bathroom door flies open and Tom enters wearing only a shirt. His expression is unreadable as he grabs my arm, sending my phone clattering to the floor.

"Let me go!" I struggle, but he's too strong. He rips the button off my trousers as he pulls them down. My throat goes dry.

Tom drapes me over the side of the bath. I squirm and wriggle, whimpering, but it's no use. "Get away from me!" My chest squeezes, restricting my airflow. I can't breathe.

Tom pulls down my boxers ripping them as if they were a piece of paper and forces his penis into me. Pain rips through my entire body and I scream. "You're hurting me!"

"Shut up," he growls in my ear. "This is what you wanted, and now you're getting it. Happy now, you fucking fat bastard?"

All the air has fled my lungs. My hands scrabble against his grip, but the pain makes me even weaker; I might as well be wrestling a tiger. Tears drip from my eyes and plop into the bathtub. The pain stretches on and on and on. I gasp for air. *Please, make it stop, make it stop, make it stop.*

Finally, after what seems like an eternity of torture, Tom pulls out. "There," he pants. "Did you enjoy that?"

"No, it hurt, and it still does."

"Get up. Get dressed."

I collapse on the bathroom floor. My body has no energy to move. I hurt all over.

"I'm going to have a ciggy," Tom announces, stalking out.

The button of my trousers rolled under the sink cupboard and I stare at it, trying to process what just happened. Did Tom make love to me, or did he rape me? Tom, my Tom, would never do anything as horrible as that. But is he really my Tom anymore?

I finally find the strength to pull myself off the cold bathroom floor and sit on the toilet seat. It's a small victory.

Tom pokes his head in through the door. "I have to go see my dad. He just called me."

I say nothing.

"Babe, come on, get dressed. I won't be long, and I thought you wanted to sort out the Christmas decorations."

"Yeah. I do." My voice comes out hollow and dead.

"Well, I can help as soon as I get back." He grins. "I know you really enjoyed that shag just then."

I talk in a shaky breath. "Is that all I am to you now? A shag? A piece of meat?"

Tom laughs and leaves. A few seconds later, I hear the front door slam. He's off to visit his dad, or to call on one of his lovers, or to get his ring back. Who knows what he's really up to?

I head into the bedroom, still shaking and crying. I grab a suitcase from inside the wardrobe and start to throw all my clothes into it. I think back to the day Tom and I first met. He seemed so nice, so handsome. The kind of person who would never dream of doing all the horrible things he's done to me. The words Lucy said during our last conversation drift back to me with startling clarity. *Tom might not be the person you think he is.* Well, it turns out, she was right. Tom is a multiple lover; he has other men in his life. And cheating on me is the least of the ways he's hurt me.

I pace the floor, turning those thoughts over and over in my head. Fact is, despite all the things Tom has done, I still love him; I can't imagine life without him. Am I giving up too easily? Am I doing the right thing?

The bedroom door opens, and I gasp and turn around. Tom smiles and waggles his hand at me. "There you go! My lovely ring is back on my finger, where it belongs."

Tom approaches and plants a kiss on my mouth. I push him off—I don't want to deal with him right now.

He raises his fist and, as a tornado on target, it crashes into my face, knocking me onto the bed. Pain erupts and expands all over my face like a nuclear mushroom cloud. I yelp and start to sob into the patterned duvet cover, pressing the blanket over my nose and mouth to protect myself.

Tom stands and looks over me as I lift my head off the duvet. My body shakes. *What is he going to do next? What is he going to do next?* The thought ricochets around in my mind, echoing over and over again.

He sits down beside me and pulls me into his slender torso. He looks past me at the suitcase on the bed. His eyebrows draw together. "You're not going anywhere."

"You have hurt, me, Tom," I say. "More than you will ever know."

He shoves his hands in his pockets. "I am sorry, babe. I am truly sorry. I haven't cheated on you, I swear. They were just old staff I used to work with and they had a party at their house last night—kind of a Coffee House reunion. That's where I was the night of BillyJeans, I promise you."

"Okay." I don't even have the energy to argue with him anymore, or consider whether he's lying or not. He takes the suitcase off the bed and starts to put my stuff back in the drawers.

I text my mum again. *Actually, I guess I'm not leaving after all.*

Tom sits on the bed and pats the spot next to him. "Sit down." I obey. He begins to kiss me, but I pull away. He says, "What's wrong?"

"I want to sort out the Christmas decorations," I say.

"Okay, babe. I am sorry, though." He kisses me again, and this time I let him. When he releases me, I get up. Time to get to work.

I set some Christmas music going and the next few hours are consumed with tinsel, lights and decorations. Despite his words earlier, Tom doesn't lift a finger to help.

He puts his feet up on the table and turns the TV on to flick through the channels. I notice a decoration on the Christmas tree that does not look placed right, and he clearly isn't going to help fix it, so I'll have to do it myself. I try to climb over his legs, but pain shoots up my body from where Tom pushed me out of the bed. I won't be able to lift my foot high enough without hurting myself.

I clear my throat. "Babe, I need to get to the tree, but you have your feet stretched out."

"Jump over them," he grunts.

My eyes widen. He has become a human barrier, for no other purpose than to make things harder for me.

As I climb over his legs to reach the Christmas tree, groaning through the pain, he turns the TV off. I reach the tree and fix the decoration and Tom snickers behind me. I turn to see him smiling at his phone, typing something back to whoever he's texting.

I climb back over his legs, gritting my teeth against the soreness and he turns his phone over as though he doesn't want me to see who he's texting. I almost ask him about it, but it could be a Christmas present he's ordering for me. I don't want to spoil the surprise.

With the flat decorated as if it was Santa's grotto, I walk over to the window and look up at the sky. A single, shining star smiles back at me. I glance at Tom, who is still on his phone. "Tom, there's a star in the sky. Come here and make a wish with me."

Tom stands up. "I'm off to bed."

My heart sinks. The old Tom would be leaping off the sofa to come and join me. Before I follow him to the bedroom, I make my wish. *'I wish the old Tom would come back to stay.*

We both head into bedroom and all I can think of is what tomorrow will bring. We lie down on the bed, he turns the bedroom light off and turns on my side, his body pressing into mine. I feel his penis erected in his boxer shorts. He starts to kiss my neck, but I lie there as stiff as a board. I can't do this. Not tonight. Not unless the old Tom comes back.

"Babe?" he mumbles into my shoulder. "Matt?"

I don't answer him, and he retreats and rolls over on his side.

The following morning, golden rays of sunlight spill into the bedroom, waking us both up. We get dressed and washed and out the door. Tom takes the car keys from my hand and smiles. "I'll drive."

He is so jolly this morning—maybe my giving him the cold shoulder last night has made him think.

We arrive at the shop, and just as we open the door, two customers approach the entrance and I let them in. A steady stream of customers flows through the shop throughout the day, and we get lost in the routine of working.

After what has been another busy day, I count the money. Tom says, "Babe, I am just having a ciggy, and then I'll be ready to go home. Hurry up."

I smile faintly and place the money in the safe. After a few other final tasks, I lock the shop up and meet Tom outside, where he is on his phone. He places it back in his pocket when he sees me and hands me the keys. I drive us home in silence.

Chapter Eight

The following day it's Christmas Eve. The town is alive with festive cheer. Tom had to go and work at the Coffee House, so I run MT Toys on my own. It's a very busy day, with lots of people buying last-minute presents for their family, so I call my mum in to help me serve everyone. I smile and wish each customer a happy Christmas, but inside I am cold.

I haven't bought Tom's Christmas presents yet, so during a brief lull I tell my mum I'm going to pop out.

"Okay, Matt love," she replies. "Don't be long, though, will you? I have shopping to do too."

I grab my coat. "I'll be back soon, Mum."

I walk at a fast pace through the town, scanning the shop windows for something that Tom might like. I spy a pair of nice shoes that are just his style and I buy those for him, along with a couple of nice shirts and a pair of jeans.

When I return, the shop is heaving. I almost panic at the thought of my poor mum trying to serve all these customers by herself, but then I spot Tom, back from the coffee shop, helping her at the counter. I sigh with relief, though I'm a little sad that my few hours of freedom away from him are over. I should hate him, but I love him with everything I've got. And that scares me.

I drop my bag of shopping in the back and relieve my mum at the till. Tom says, "Where did you go, Matt?"

"I just had to pop out to buy some last remaining presents. You finished work early."

"Yeah, we closed early. Fiona has to travel up to London and she didn't want to get caught up in the Christmas traffic." He smiles at a customer as he scans her items. "But that reminds me, I have to go buy some things too. Are all the shops still open?"

"I think so," I reply. "All except for the Coffee House, apparently," as I wink at him.

My mother grabs her coat and kisses me and Tom. We both thank her for helping us today.

"See you both for dinner tomorrow!" she says, walking out the door. Tom leaves with her.

I gaze out the window as my mother walks up the street with Tom. The light outside is fading and the rush of customers will be fading to a trickle, soon.

At about four o'clock, the last customer leaves and I decide to close up for the Christmas season. I'm just changing the 'Open' sign to 'Closed' when Harry appears at the door.

"Closing already, Matt?" he says.

"Yes, Harry. It's Christmas."

"Well, Merry Christmas to you both, I suppose. Where's the other half?"

"Gone to buy some last-minute gifts."

Harry snorts. "I bet all the good stuff will be gone by now."

"Well, we can only hope." I shake Harry's hand and he leaves.

I go to the back room of the shop and wrap Tom's presents on the table. We have some very nice black carrier bags to use for gifts, so I select one and put the presents inside. As I grab my coat, there's a knock on the door. I return to the front to see Tom standing outside.

I open the door. "Just closed up, babe."

Tom leans forward and kisses me. "Excellent. Come on. Let's start our Christmas."

I say, "Yep."

We lock up the shop and walk up the street, me with my large black bag and Tom with his shopping bags. Most of the shops are closed, but the pubs and restaurants are alive with people. We pass the Christmas tree and I giggle. "Remember when Harry was complaining to us about where they were putting the tree?"

"Yeah," Tom says. "Looks like he got his wish after all."

We drive home and settle in for an early night.

Tom pushes me onto the sofa. Our tongues dance with one another and my heart sings—has the old, kind, sweet Tom returned?

He runs his hands down my body, kissing every part, and I'm in heaven until he touches a bruise still hasn't fully healed. I wince at the pain, but he kisses it tenderly. I unbutton my trousers and wrench them off, tossing them and my underwear on the carpet. Tom wastes no time in stripping himself and he lies on top of me, the warm tip of his penis touching my thigh.

Tom makes love to me on the sofa for the first time since the bathroom incident, but this time he is gentle as a teddy bear. Why couldn't it be like this all the time? Why did Tom have to hurt me to get what he wanted? And why did he sleep with other men when he could've just stuck with me? He said he didn't cheat, but I'm not convinced. It hardly matters now. I don't know that I could leave him if I tried.

Afterwards, we lie on the sofa, hugging and kissing one and another, our skin damp with sweat.

Tom says, "I just need to go and have a ciggy."

"Okay. I'm going to bed."

"Keep my side of the bed warm for me."

I reply, "I will."

I hide Tom's presents underneath the tree by covering them with branches and tinsel. I switch the living room light off, walk back to the bedroom and get under the covers.

Not very long after, Tom joins me and hugs me and kisses me goodnight. "I love you."

"I love you," I echo.

We drift off to sleep.

*

It's the dawning of Christmas Day and I am wide awake the second my eyes open. Tom is still fast asleep, so I slowly get out of bed, careful not to wake him.

My thoughts go back to how Tom made love to me last night on the sofa and how amazing it felt. I feel so blessed to have the old Tom back. I'm sure he's sorry for all the hurt he has caused me, and it was all just a fluke that won't happen again. This is going to be the best Christmas of all time!

I make my way into the living room and switch the Christmas lights on. The bulbs join with the morning sunlight to brighten up the entire room. I bend down in front of the tree and bring Tom's presents forward. Some of the baubles catch the light and cast rainbow patterns on the carpet and ceiling. It's perfect.

My phone pings with a text from my mother. *Merry Christmas to you and Tom! The turkey is in the oven. Don't be late!*

I text her back, wishing her, Dad and Loraine a Merry Christmas too. I flick on the telly and watch Christmas specials for a few hours. When the clock hits ten, I decide to go check on Tom and get dressed. I find him sitting up in bed, typing on his phone. He turns it off and throws it face down on the bedside table. "Merry Christmas, Matt." I'm expecting him to try and kiss me, but he doesn't.

I push all the strangeness aside—I can't spend Christmas Day worrying about who Tom might be texting. "My mum wants us there for dinner at twelve."

"Okay."

"Are you getting up to open your presents?"

"Yeah, in a minute." He fiddles with a loose thread on the duvet.

"Well, don't be long. You've got less than two hours till we have to leave."

He says, "Yes, Matt, I know."

I return to the living room and get back to the Christmas specials. An hour later, Tom joins me, already dressed for Christmas dinner. He kisses me and our tongues lock together. His hands start to wander, but I stop him. "We won't have time to open your presents."

"I'll open them later."

"Well, I still need to get ready for dinner."

"Okay, fine." He grabs the remote and flicks through the channels on the TV. I head to the bathroom to get ready. As I catch sight of the bathtub, my memory flicks to that horrible morning when Tom bent me over the bathtub. The pain is still fresh in my mind. I barely manage to avoid cutting myself with my razor as I attempt to shave with shaking hands.

As I straighten my tie, the door opens. I jump with fright and let out a squeak.

Tom pauses in the doorway. "Are you all right, babe? Did I scare you?"

"Yes." I drop my eyes to the washbasin.

"Sorry, babe." He lifts my face and kisses me. I try not to think about him forcing himself inside me in this very room.

"Can you get my family's presents?" I ask. "They're under the tree."

"Sure." He gives me one last peck and leaves. I try to breathe easy again.

As I leave the bathroom, my eyes wander over to the bathtub and my mind suddenly flashes with the memory of Tom raping me, my lungs squeezing with panic, my body convulsing in pain. I dart from the bathroom and slam the door, the trapped breeze floating out. I gasp, trying to compose myself. It's Christmas, I should be happy! I force myself to dance down the stairs with a Christmas tune in my head.

I open the front door and Tom has the engine running. The radio blasts a festive song as I slide into the front seat. We both sing along on the journey to my parents and I pretend that maybe, just maybe, everything is normal.

When we arrive at my parents' house, my dad greets us at the door with a hug. My mother is busy dishing up the dinner in the kitchen, but she pauses to give me a kiss and wish me a Merry Christmas. I'm helping her arrange the finger sandwiches on a plate when I realise Tom has disappeared.

I poke my head out of the kitchen to see Tom talking on the phone in the hallway. I hear him say into the phone, "You know I like your lips around my cock."

He glances up when he sees me, opens the front door and continues the call outside.

There's no time to worry, though, because my mother calls to me to help her bring the dinner into the dining room.

Tom comes back inside and sits down at the table just in time. My mum bends over to kiss him on the cheek. "Merry Christmas, Tom!"

"Yeah, Merry Christmas." He smiles at her, but it doesn't reach his eyes.

My sister bursts through the concertina doors and takes her place at the table. "Merry Christmas, Matt! Merry Christmas, Tom!" Her eyes go wide as she looks at the food. "Wow, Mum, you've really outdone yourself this time!"

"All right, let's eat!" my dad says.

I watch Tom as the rest of us tuck into Mum's delicious spread. Aside from nibbling on his turkey, he leaves his food untouched. My mother tries to make conversation with him, but he only answers with one-word responses or grunts.

After dinner, we head to the living room to play charades, pull Christmas crackers and tell jokes. Tom sits in the corner of the sofa the whole time, refusing to participate in any activities. What's the matter with him? Could it be something to do with that phone call he didn't want me to hear?

My mother catches my eye. "Matt, love, I want to start washing a few dishes before the evening is over. Would you come and help me?"

"Sure, Mum." I follow her into the kitchen.

Mum leans against the counter, blatantly ignoring the dirty dishes. "Matt, are you and Tom getting along okay?"

For a second, I almost tell her about everything. But it's only recently that things started going downhill. Things were perfect before then—and maybe with time, they'll be perfect again. They have to be, because I can't live without Tom.

"Yes, Mum, we're fine."

She studies me for a few seconds and then seems satisfied. "All right, then. Let's open presents."

We return to the living room, where I hand my parents and my sister their presents from me and Tom. Just as they're ripping the wrapping paper off, Tom looks at the time on his phone. "Matt, we have to be going," he mutters. "I want to go and visit my dad."

"Okay, Tom. In a few minutes."

"No!" His lip curls slightly. "Now, Matt!"

Shock flits across my mum's face, but she composes herself enough to say, "Okay, boys, if you have to leave then you have to leave. You both have a lovely Christmas. What's left of it, anyway? All this build-up for one day and then it's gone. See you both for dinner tomorrow."

My mum hugs me and kisses me on the cheek. Tom walks off to the car with his ciggy and his phone, not even waiting for my mum to say goodbye to him.

"Are you sure everything is okay, love?" my mum whispers to me.

"Yes, Mum. I think he is just worried about his dad." I wish I felt half as confident as I sound.

My mother and father wave me off and I head to the car with our still-wrapped presents under my arm. I slide into the passenger seat. Tom grips the wheel, a nasty expression contorting his face. How can someone who's usually so beautiful become so ugly? And what did I do to make him so angry?

Tom drives us to the flat without saying a word.

As we drive back to our flat, Tom's phone rings. I say to him, "Shall I answer it for you?"

He grunts, and the silence stretches out for several seconds before he says, "Yeah."

The number is withheld. I accept the call and put the phone to my ear. Music plays in the background, loud and upbeat, and the voice at the other end says, "Oi, Tom, it's Mart. We still on for our shag tomorrow night?"

The breath flies out of my lungs and I couldn't answer even if I wanted to. I jab my finger into the "end call" button. Tom glances at me as tears start to fill my eyes. Something wet trickles down my cheek. I gasp for air, the walls of the car closing in on me like a vice.

Tom slams on the brakes, so hard that my seatbelt almost winds me. "What's the fucking matter, Matt? I said, what's the fucking matter?"

I can't find the words to speak. My voice fled the second I heard the words of the guy at the end of the phone asking Tom if they were still on for their shag tomorrow. The voice still reverberates in my mind. As I glance out of the window, I see Tom pulling his arm back in the reflection of the glass, and I've barely processed what he's doing when his fist smashes into the side of my face. My head hits the passenger door window and my brain fills with clouds for a second. I burst into tears, a burning sensation filling my skull. "What was that for, Tom?" I scream.

Tom presses his lips together and speeds onwards, tyres squealing on the road.

By the time we arrive home, I am still trembling in my seat. Tom leans over and wraps his arms around me, pressing a kiss to my aching temple. "I am sorry, Matt."

I reply, "Are you, Tom?"

He does not say anything.

He gets out the second he turns the car off, leaving me to carry all the presents. I climb the stairs and enter the living room to find Tom ripping the paper off one of the presents I bought for him, balancing his phone on his shoulder as he listens to someone talking on the other end.

I set the gifts from my parents on the coffee table. "Okay, we can open presents now. Good idea. Where are mine?"

Tom points to a carrier bag under the tree. I glance inside it to find a few cheap-looking presents, none of which are wrapped.

For some reason, all I can fixate on is the lack of wrapping paper. Funny what your mind focuses on when you're slowly falling to pieces. "Why didn't you wrap them?" I ask him.

Tom takes the phone from his ear and hangs up his call. "I never had time. Just fucking have them, or don't bother." He shoves his now-opened present—the pair of shoes I bought him—underneath the coffee table.

"Tom, what's wrong? You've been in a funny mood all day. Even my parents noticed it."

Tom stands up. "I'm going for a pee." He places his phone screen-down on the coffee table as he leaves.

I quickly pick his phone up before the screen locks. A message thread is up from someone called Martin. As I scroll, my eyes get wider and wider, taking in vivid descriptions of all the dirty things Martin wants to do to my boyfriend—and things that my boyfriend wants to do to him. The most recent messages confirm that Tom has arranged to meet Martin tomorrow night on the bench in the park.

The toilet flushes, but my muscles have frozen me in place. I stare at the screen, tears blurring my vision, until the phone switches off on its own.

Tom's footsteps sound behind me. My voice quavers as I say, "Who's Martin?"

"No one." Tom snatches the phone out of my hand.

"You've been cheating on me again."

"What the fuck are you on about? You're crazy."

I struggle to keep speaking around the lump in my throat. "It's all on your fucking phone. You have been sleeping with him behind my back. It's written right there." I place my finger on the screen and point at the message on Tom's phone. "And there was that call I answered while you were driving. You can't deny it!"

He looks away, but not before I see a truly furious expression erupting across his face. His jaw tics. Tom's fist crashes into my head, once, twice, three times. My head rings and I flail my arms, trying to fight him off as the blows keep coming. What is happening? Something warm trickles from my nose. I crumple under Tom's onslaught. That's it; I'm going to die here, killed by the man I love.

No, I can't let that happen. I can't die. I let out a yell and shove Tom as hard as I possibly can. He stumbles back, sitting down hard on the sofa. I get to my feet, pinching my nose shut as blood stains my fingers.

Tom snarls and dives for the shoes under the coffee table. He grabs one and launches it into the side of my head. "Fuck!" I scream, pressing my other hand to the site of the new blossoming pain. I stagger to the armchair and sit down, bracing myself for another round.

Luckily, Tom just gets up and storms off to the bedroom, slamming the door behind him.

I remain frozen in the chair, shaking, waiting for Tom to return. After an eternity, I realise he's probably gone to sleep. I should too, but as exhausted as I am, I can't relax.

The hands on the clock revolve with military precision. Boxing Day dawns with a weak, watery light. I gaze out the window. What will today bring? Good Tom, or Bad Tom?

I stretch my arms and my head throbs. I get up and gaze at my reflection in the mirror. More bruises, a small cut above my ear and trails of blackish dried blood.

The horror hits me all at once. Tom, my Tom, the man I love, threw a shoe at me, beat me with his fists until I was sure I would die. It seemed like a horrible dream, but as I search the bathroom cabinets for something, anything, to put on my battered face, I realise that this is reality. My bitter reality that stares back at me, bruised and bloodied, from the mirror. I can't erase the marks of a Christmas spent in fear and tears.

There's nothing useful in the bathroom, but there might be something in our bedside drawers. I make my way silently to the bedroom and slowly open the door so I don't wake Tom. He's all wrapped up in the duvet and he looks like he is still sleeping peacefully. I hold my breath so as not to wake him as I kneel beside the bed and quietly open the first drawer. Nothing there, so I ease the second drawer open. Success! I take the ointment and slip it into my pocket. "What the fuck are you looking for?" Tom roars.

I am glued to the spot, frozen in fear. How can I feel like this about a man I love so much? I blubber out a few apologies, but I realise I have to tell him the truth. Maybe then he will see, just once, how much he has hurt me. "I needed some antiseptic cream for my head. You threw shoes at my face yesterday. I'm all cut and bruised."

I wait for an apology, any sign he is sorry, but instead Tom picks his phone up and looks at the screen. "It's nine fucking a.m.! Are you nuts?"

I cower. "It's not that early, babe. I have been-awake hours." I laugh weakly at my useless attempt at a joke. But Tom can hear weakness.

He strikes, raising his arms and hitting me in the face. All the blows last night made me feel empty, but somehow this one completely shatters my world. The floodgates open, pouring more tears than I ever thought possible out of my eyes. I gaze up at Tom, begging, pleading. "Why? Why would you do this?" But I could be talking to a stranger in the street. The face before me belongs to the man I love, but that's where the resemblance ends. The person behind it is not my Tom. Instead, he's a wicked, cold, unfeeling void. I have never felt so alone.

Trying to gather myself from the floor, I fumble for words to say; words to make him hear me, hear my pain, understand that my heart is breaking. "You hurt me. I am sorry I woke you, but I was just trying to find something to put onto my face."

Judging by his unfeeling mask of an expression, I might as well be throwing my words into a bottomless well. I swallow. This is truly the worst Christmas ever in the history of Christmases.

I get up on shaking legs. I have to get out of this room. But before I can go, Tom slides out of bed and raises a fist.

I shrink against the wall, but the blow never comes. Instead, he snarls, "Get the fuck out of *my* room, you overgrown fucking fat whale!"

Every word is like a dagger to my heart, shattering me beyond repair. I slip away and sprint to the bathroom. Behind me, he shouts, "Wake me up again and there will be another bruise to match the one you got yesterday!" A small object whooshes past my head and the bedroom door slams.

I stand in front of my bathroom mirror, wincing as I apply the cream to my face. *Who am I? How did this happen? Why?* The simple questions race around my mind, their simple answers eluding me. My mind simply refuses to work the way it's supposed to. Tom has broken me, and yet I can't fathom the idea of leaving him.

A ping from my phone drags me back to reality. It's my mum, asking if Tom and I are still coming for our family's traditional Boxing Day meal. I can't let her down, so I reply that we shall see her at 1 p.m.

I hear another ping, but it doesn't come from my phone. I head out into the living room to see Tom's device on the carpet. I remember when I was fleeing the bedroom and he threw something at me—it must have been his phone. The notification on the screen is a text from Jack.

I pick up the phone and press the home button out of habit. To my surprise, the screen unlocks. Tom must have turned the passcode off. Why would he do that?

My mouth falls open as I look at the nude photo that Jack just sent. As I watch, another one pops up. It slowly dawns on me—Tom removed his passcode because he doesn't care about secrecy anymore. He wants me to know what he's getting up to with other men, just to torture me; how could he be so brutal to me?

The phone slips from my fingers and thumps back onto the carpet. I wander to the sofa and pick up a magazine. I need to do something to stop myself thinking about all the horrors of the last twenty-four hours. I hum a little tune, flicking to an article that might interest me. But before I can even start pretending that everything is okay, the bedroom door flies open.

Tom walks towards me, half-dressed, and I can see from the look on his face that he is furious. My stomach ties in knots; I think I'm going to be sick.

"I told you to be fucking quiet!" he rages.

I fumble for words, half-formed apologies dying on my lips, but Tom continues his rant. "I'm sick of having to share this fucking flat with you. You make me miserable. I am heading to BillyJeans tonight and getting drunk. I don't want your fat fucking face there."

"Okay." I try to smile. "I…I mean, you've seemed stressed lately, and I'm sure some relaxation will do you some good."

"I don't fucking care what you think. I don't want to relax; I want to forget. Forget you and your pathetic shit." He punches me in the face and I crumble to the floor, the pain from the blow taking me to my knees. Tom storms out and I press my hands to my head. Again, the tears come, and I don't stop them.

In a rage, he lifts the Christmas tree from its stand and throws it against the wall. The coloured effulgent baubles smash and shatter into pieces on the living room floor. He picks up a Christmas figurine and stamps on it until it's broken into bits. He leaves the living room and walks back into the bedroom to put the remainder of his clothes on.

Tom comes back into the room fully dressed, and for a second, I entertain a sliver of hope that he will apologise. But this is the bad new Tom; not my Tom. He looks down on me as I hold my head. "I can't do this anymore I need to get out of here."

I look up at the face I love, which somehow manages to be beautiful and ugly at the same time. "What do you mean?"

"Be with you! I have to get out of here. I never really wanted to be with you; I just took pity on you because you're a complete fucking idiot; even Dan and Paul said I could get better. I needed someone to cook, clean and iron for me and you were one."

Through my tears, I beg to know what I did, beg him to tell me how this happened, but my words just enrage him. He kicks me in my leg and my ribs explode. I gasp for breath and curl into a ball, crumpled and broken on the floor.

"Oh yeah, and when I was making love to you, I had to pretend I was making love to all those other guys who were a better shag than you could ever be. I'd never be able to get off otherwise." His spittle hits my face. "That's right, Matt. I never really cared about you—you were just a safety net. But

I don't need you anymore. Have a good lonely life, you fat bastard."

Tom turns and runs out of the room, down the stairs and out the door, slamming it behind him.

I try to stand, but my body is too damaged to move. I slowly gain the strength and drag myself across the living room, towards the landing. "Tom? Tom?" My voice comes out weak and pathetic. It's no use; my weak voice just echoes in the empty hallway.

I look at my phone to check the time. It's 9:30 am. We'll have to start getting ready to go to Mum's in a few hours. Funny what your brain focuses on when you're falling apart.

I make my way into the bedroom. All of Tom's clothes are still there, including the Christmas presents I gave him yesterday. But the Christmas cards from mine and his family, which contained gift cards and money, are gone. My heart sinks with shock.

As I search through the drawers full of both my and Tom's clothes, I find a large pile of papers stuffed under a pile of his trousers. I turn them over, and they're not just papers—they're photographs. The first one shows Tom standing in BillyJeans with his arm around the waist of a handsome man I've never seen before.

My throat constricts as I shuffle through the rest of the pictures. The background of BillyJeans remains the same, but each one displays Tom with a different guy—holding him close, kissing him on the lips. One photo, of Tom making out with a thin blond man, makes me do a double take—that woman with the dark hair in the background looks a lot like Lucy, and the man she's talking to is definitely Lewis. I choke back a sob. Lucy was right all along about Tom.

I drift back into the living room. It's started to snow outside. I stare at the white flakes, my body aching, tears rolling down my face. With every bit of strength, I have left in my aching body, I remove the ring Tom placed back on my finger a few days ago and place it on the table next to a photograph of us both in happier times, still staring out of the window as the snow turns the cold stone pavements and roads into a winter wonderland.

I realise Tom's gone.

The End